UNITED NATIONS CONFERENCE ON TRADE AND DEVELOPMENT

UNCTAD

CHINA'S STRUCTURAL TRANSFORMATION
WHAT CAN DEVELOPING COUNTRIES LEARN?

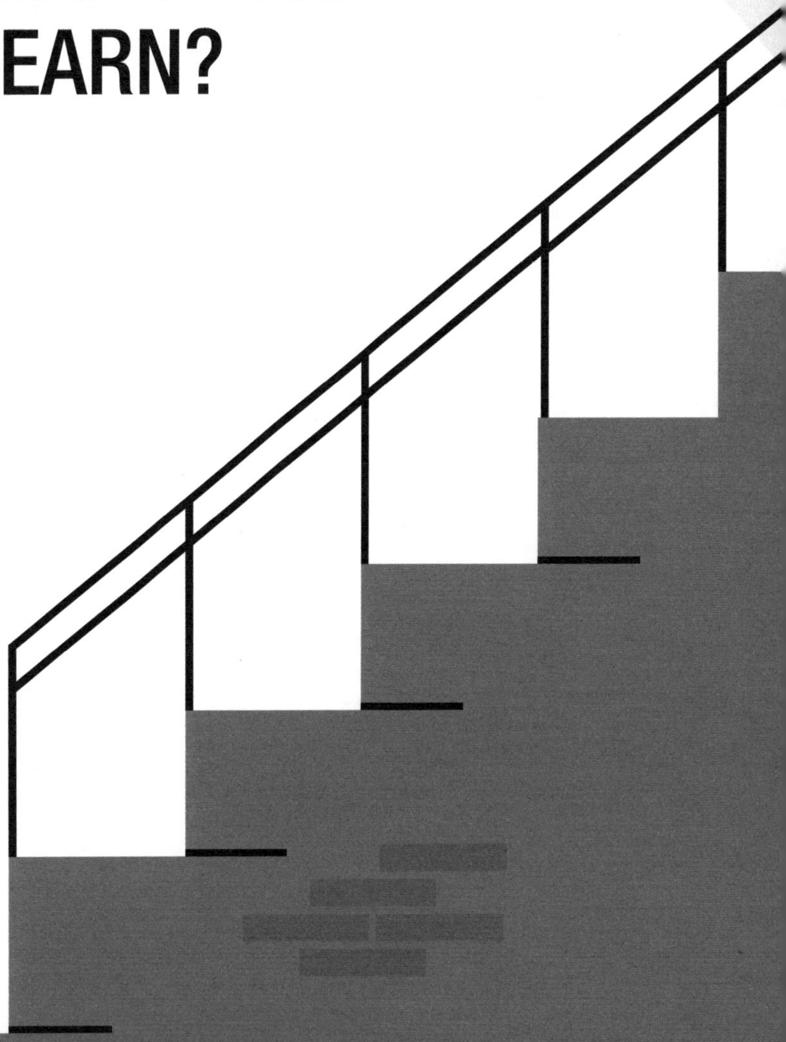

UNITED NATIONS

Geneva, 2022

United Nations Publications
405 East 42nd Street
New York, New York 10017
United States of America
Email: publications@un.org
Website: https://shop.un.org/

United Nations publication issued by the
United Nations Conference on Trade and Development.

UNCTAD/GDS/2022/1
Sales No. E.22.II.D.9
ISBN: 978-92-1-113037-9 eISBN: 978-92-1-001446-5

Foreword

Over the past four decades, China has achieved remarkable economic growth, lifting millions out of poverty and meeting major international development goals, contributing significantly to the 2030 Agenda for Sustainable Development. In the process China has transformed itself from a global assembly hub to a global digital leader. What is the policy story behind China's "economic miracle"? What strategies lie behind its successful integration into the global economy? What kind of reference point can it offer to other developing countries through South-South policy experience sharing?

This volume sets out to provide some answers to these questions through a series of studies on the Chinese "economic miracle". It focuses on several complementary policy areas that provide key insights in explaining the rapid growth trajectory of China, namely, macroeconomic and finance, industrial development, international trade and the digital economy. The book has greatly benefited from the discussions that took place in the two international workshops held in Beijing and Jakarta in 2019 and several webinars organized under the project in close cooperation with partner organizations including China's Development and Research Center (DRC), China's Academy of International Trade and Economic Cooperation (CAITEC), Indonesia's Institute for Development of Economics and Finance (INDEF), Ethiopia's Policy Study Institute (PSI) and Sri Lanka' Information and Communication Technology Agency (ICTA), with the participation of key actors from the public institutions, academia and the private sector.

This book contributes to the existing literature on China's structural transformation. It also provides developing countries with an important learning opportunity on policies that can help them progress towards the sustainable development goals.

The volume has been prepared in the framework of the project titled "South-South Integration and The SDGs: Enhancing Structural Transformation in Key Partner Countries of the Belt and Road Initiative" funded by UNPDF Sub-Fund for SDG. The project is being implemented by the Division of Globalization and Development Strategies of UNCTAD since 2018 and aims at encouraging peer-learning.

Richard Kozul-Wright
Director, Division on Globalization and Development Strategies
UNCTAD

Acknowledgements

This book has been prepared under UNCTAD's project on "South-South Integration and The SDGs: Enhancing Structural Transformation in Key Partner Countries of the Belt and Road Initiative" funded by UNPDF Sub-Fund for SDG. The team comprised Rashmi Banga, Piergiuseppe Fortunato, Ricardo Gottschalk, Penelope Hawkins and Dawei Wang. The authors are grateful to the consultants from China who prepared the policy papers. These papers are available on UNCTAD's website at: https://unctad.org/topic/south-south-cooperation/bri-platform. The authors are also grateful to all the participants of the conferences/webinars organised under the project for their valuable comments and suggestions. We thank Florence Hudry and Adriana Sofia Diaz Fuenmayor for formatting the book and Marina Zucker Marques for copyediting this book.

Table of Contents

List of Figures

List of Tables

CHAPTER 1
Introduction

Chapter 1: Introduction

1.1 Covid-19 and the Multiple Development Challenges Facing the South

The Covid-19 pandemic has created new development challenges for the South. Millions of people are losing their jobs and being pushed into extreme poverty. The global economy contracted by 3.9 per cent in 2020 (UNCTAD, 2021) and 255 million full-time jobs were lost (ILO (2021).[1] Developing countries have not only been hit harder economically by this crisis but will also take more time to recover because of their limited financial resources (UNCTAD, 2020).[2] The World Bank (2021) estimates that globally the Covid-19 crisis has added between 119 to 124 million new poor, with around 60 per cent of them living in South Asia.[3]

While rapid vaccination can lead to faster recovery on the health front, economic recovery will require additional financial resources and policy support. Billions of dollars are being rolled out by developed countries to revive their economies. According to UNCTAD (2020), on average developed countries have spent 30 per cent of their GDP on economic recovery measures, while developing countries spent less than 5 per and least developed countries only 1 per cent. With limited financial resources, developing countries will need to revisit their macro-economic, financial, trade, and industrial policies. Developing countries need not only to recover faster from the pandemic but also 'recover better,' with more equitable and sustainable growth. Achieving this goal would require refocusing their policies on the structural transformation of their economies.

However, very few developing countries have been able to achieve structural transformation, especially with the onset of the fourth digital industrial revolution. China is one example: it has evolved from an agrarian economy to the world's manufacturing hub and now has emerged as one of the global digital leaders.

1.2 Has China Structurally Transformed Itself?

While it can be said that China has successfully transformed itself from an agrarian economy to a digital economy, whether China has achieved structural transformation or not is still an open question. Structural transformation is a multidimensional concept and has been defined in many ways. A normative definition of structural transformation is "the movement of a country's productive resources (natural resources, land, capital, labour, and know-how) from

---

[1] World Employment and Social Outlook: Trends 2021 (WESO Trends).

[2] https://unctad.org/system/files/official-document/gdsinf2020d4_en.pdf

[3] https://blogs.worldbank.org/opendata/updated-estimates-impact-covid-19-global-poverty-looking-back-2020-and-outlook-2021#:~:text=The%20COVID%2D19%20pandemic%20is,(downside%20estimate)%20in%202020.

low-productivity to high-productivity economic activities" (Monga and Lin, 2019: 1); or "the ability of an economy to constantly generate new dynamic activities characterized by higher productivity and increasing returns to scale" (UNIDO, 2013: 16). However, beyond analyzing compositional changes, it is also necessary to assess whether they were accompanied by: (i) diversification of output and exports; (ii) rising labour productivity; (iii) convergence of the level of labour productivity of different economic sectors (McMillan and Rodrik, 2011); (iv) higher income per capita; and (v) substantive poverty reduction. These structural changes also need to be sustainable and should not lead to premature deindustrialization.

1.2.1 Challenge of Inequitable Growth

Figure 1.1: Gini coefficient, China, 2012–2018

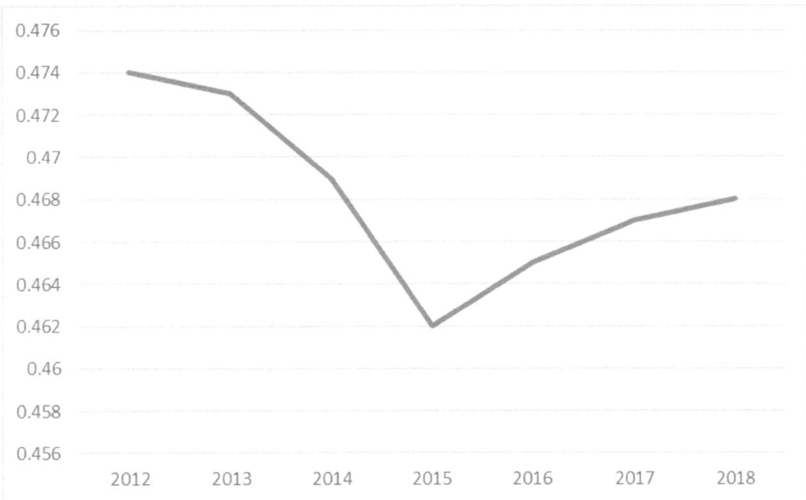

Source: National Bureau of Statistics of China.

Figure 1.2: Rural-urban per capita disposable income gap, China, 1990–2018, (thousand yuan)

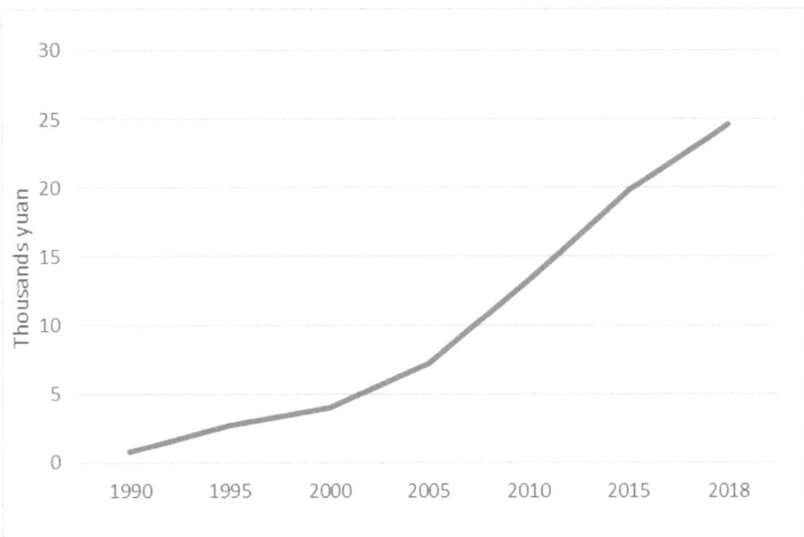

Source: National Bureau of Statistics of China.

In the case of China, we find that GDP has recorded an average annual growth rate of 9.3 per cent from 1990 to 2019, with an average GDP per capita growth of 9 per cent annually. While 30 per cent of the population was below the national poverty line in 2005, this ratio declined to 0.6 per cent in 2019. In early 2021, China announced that it has eradicated extreme poverty based on the national poverty line. Pulling millions of people out of poverty was accompanied by other structural transformation indicators, including the declining agriculture, forestry, and fishing value-added as a percentage of GDP from 27 per cent in 1990 to 7 per cent in 2019. At the same time, the value-added by the manufacturing sector declined from 41 to 39 per cent, while value-added by services increased from 32 per cent to 54 per cent (World Development Indicators). The unemployment rate dropped from 4.1 per cent in 2015 to 3.6 per cent in 2019. Further, employment in the tertiary sector increased from 23 per cent in 1994 to 46 per cent in 2018. In the same period, employment in agriculture declined from 54 per cent to 26 per cent (National Bureau of Statistics of China).

However, despite China's titanic growth, which made it the second-largest economy in the world, the country still faces many developmental challenges. Among them, rising income inequality is one of the most daunting ones. Inequality measured by Gini Coefficient[4] has been increasing in China since 2015 (figure 1), along with a rising gap in per capita disposable income between rural and urban households.

1.2.2 Industrial Growth with Rising Labour Productivity

Figure 1.1: Industrial growth and value-added per worker, China, 1992–2020

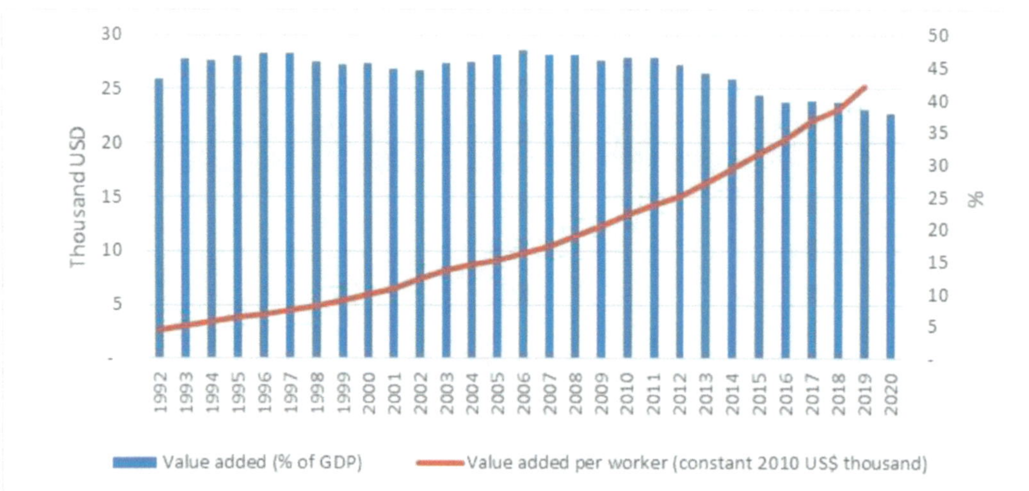

Source: World Development Indicators.

Despite rising inequality, the industrial growth rate in China has been exemplary. Between 1992 and 2020, industrial value-added grew on average 11 per cent annually. While industrial

[4] Gini coefficient measures the extent to which the distribution of income within an economy deviates from a perfectly equal distribution.

value-added represented 41 per cent of GDP in 1992, this ratio rose to 47 per cent in 2012 and declined to 39 in 2020 (Figure 3). Value-added per worker in the industry grew steadily from USD 2,245 in 1992 to USD 25,272 in constant terms in 2020. During this period, the share of medium and high-tech industries (including construction) as a percentage of manufacturing value-added also remained as high as 40 per cent on average.

1.2.3 Growing Share in the International Trade and Global Value Chains

Industrial growth in China was accompanied by a fast-rising share of China's exports in international trade. The ratio of merchandise trade to GDP rapidly increased: from an average of 10 per cent in the 1970s to 25 per cent in the 1980s and 37 per cent in the 1990s. It reached an average of 53 per cent in the 2000s and then declined to 38 per cent from 2011 to 2019. Trade in services to GDP ratio, in its turn, has remained much lower: between 6 to 8 per cent during these periods.[5]

It is essential to note that while international trade has remained one of the key drivers of China's growth, China has strived to increase its domestic value-added content in its exports. Using Trade-in-Value Added (TiVA database by OECD-2018), it is estimated that the foreign value-added content in China's exports declined by 9.6 percentage points between 2005 and 2016, suggesting a rise in domestic sourcing for exports.

China has emerged as a major player in forming global value chains, especially engaging southeast Asia. The trading partners with high shares of China's value-added in their manufacturing exports to China in 2015 were Viet Nam, Malaysia, and Cambodia, respectively. Services' contribution to the Chinese economy is also rising rapidly, and accordingly, its contribution to manufacturing exports has increased over the years. In 2015, services value-added content in China's gross manufacturing exports was 29.7 per cent, with the highest share of ICT and electronics sectors.

1.2.4 Digital Transformation

With the advent of the fourth digital industrial revolution, China has emerged as one of the global digital leaders. The digital economy has contributed to nearly 60 per cent of China's GDP growth in 2016, becoming the new driver of its economic growth. In 2016, while China's digital economy was still only 32 per cent of the size of the US economy, accounting for 30 per cent of its GDP, its annual growth rate was close to 19 per cent -more than three times that of the US (6 per cent). In terms of the ICT Development Index, given its large population, China was ranked 80th in 176 countries in 2017, with 55.5 per cent of households with internet access (with Asia Pacific average being 45.5 per cent). China has also made rapid progress in other digital development indicators, especially digital infrastructure, digital technologies, and e-commerce. The speed of fixed broadband in China increased more than three times in 2018

[5] World Development Indicators, 2021.

compared to 2015, while the average mobile data tariff declined more than nine times in this period.[6]

In terms of Big Data analytics and AI, China has made rapid progress and is now catching up with the US. According to *Worldwide Semi-Annual Big Data and Analytics Spending Guide* from International Data Cooperation (IDC), the Big Data market in the Asia Pacific reached US$ 14.7 billion in 2018, of which China has the most significant market with a spending of US$ 5.5 billion. While AI is still in its nascent stages in many developing countries, China has made AI its national priority and is rapidly expanding its AI industry. China is developing a technology park in Beijing worth $ 2.1 billion and has announced plans to develop its AI industry,[7] which will generate $ 60 billion annual output by 2025 and will become a $150 billion industry by 2030. One of the fastest-growing digital technology is robotics. In 2016, with 87,000 industrial robots, China surpassed the US and Germany. China has also recorded the fastest growth in its robot density (increasing from 25 in 2013 to 68 in 2016- IFR, 2018).

In terms of e-commerce, China has experienced the fastest growth in the world. By 2018, China's cross-border e-commerce (CBEC) reached 740 million buyers, increasing by an annual compound growth rate of 96%, which greatly exceeds the global CBEC (54.1%) and of the entire e-commerce industry (31.5%). In 2020, imports and exports of China's cross-border e-commerce totaled 1.69 trillion yuan ($261.5 billion), up 31 per cent year-on-year, according to the General Administration of Customs (GAC).[8] E-commerce exports increased by 40 per cent yearly, while imports increased by 16.5 per cent. China's e-commerce platforms have also grown in number and size, with rising profits over the years.

1.2.5 Strong Macro-Economic Fundamentals and Rising Debt to GDP Ratio

The digital transformation of China has gone together with strong macro-economic fundamentals. China's external position has remained solid, with a surplus in the current account every year since 1994. The capital account has followed suit in most years, while the trade balance has also remained positive, reaching USD 421 billion in 2019. As a result, China's foreign exchange reserves increase stupendously from USD 165 billion in 2001 to USD 3.14 trillion in 2018. Total reserves as a percentage of total external debt increased from 119 in 2001 to 152 in 2019, with net foreign assets rising by 900 per cent during this period.[9]

Foreign direct investment inflows have increased steadily in China, as have the FDI outflows. FDI inflows increased by USD 27 trillion between 2010 to 2019, while FDI outflows increased by USD 49 trillion. During 2016–19, China continued to open its fixed income markets (for both corporate and government securities) to foreign investors and took further measures to reduce non-residents restrictions on equity market flows.

---

[6] Ministry of Industry and Information Technology (MIIT).

[7] http://www.xinhuanet.com/english/2018-01/03/c_136869144.htm

[8] https://www.globaltimes.cn/page/202101/1212876.shtml

[9] https://www.focus-economics.com/countries/china

Strong growth in China did not result in high inflation rates, contrary to what has been historically seen in developing countries. China's average annual Consumer price index (CPI) growth during 1978-2019 was 4.9 per cent, much below other developing countries like India and Brazil in this period. In 2019, the inflation rate remained at a manageable level of 2.9 per cent, below the world's average of 3.1 per cent and well below the 5.5 per cent in developing countries.

However, even with strong macro-economic fundamentals, China's total debt to GDP ratio has surged over the years, rising from 120 per cent in 1997 to over 300 per cent in 2019. Corporate and household debt have grown much faster than government debt leading to increasing worries about China's debt sustainability.

1.3 Learning from China's Growth Process

Despite its challenges, China's growth process has successfully pulled millions of people out of poverty, reduced unemployment, increased labour productivity and enhanced digital skills and capacities. While China's growth experience cannot be replicated, it provides valuable lessons and learnings for other developing countries, especially during the post-pandemic period, when developing countries need to revisit their macro-economic, financial, trade, and industrial policies to recover better with equitable and resilient growth. China's digital policies have been highly successful in digitally transforming the country and, therefore, can provide important blueprints for designing digital policies in developing countries, particularly those which have initiated the designing their national data policies.

Further, the pandemic has raised concerns regarding debt sustainability in many developing countries. Although China's rising debt to GDP ratio is primarily driven by debt to state-owned non-financial, which is not common to many developing countries, China's increasing non-financial corporate debt does not provide an external constraint. Furthermore, it has been channelled by local governments into fiscally sustainable infrastructure investment, which is expected to boost medium to long term growth. Many developing countries facing debt-sustainability issues can draw important lessons from China's policy regarding its debt sustainability.

Given China's successful growth experience, this book aims to share and build awareness concerning China's macro-economic, financial, industrial, and trade policies- mainly focusing on global value chains, digital policies, and debt sustainability. Developing countries can draw practical policy lessons by adjusting them to their ground realities.

The book is organized as follows: chapter 2 discusses China's macroeconomic and financial policies and draws lessons for developing countries; Chapter 3 examines China's industrial policy experience since 1978 and highlights those policies which facilitated its industrialization process; chapter 4 highlights China's policies which helped in upgrading in the global value chains and successfully integrating into the world economy; Chapter 5 shares China's digital policies which helped in its digital transformation; chapter 6 provides insights into China's approach to internal and external debts and draws lessons for developing countries for debt sustainability.

CHAPTER 2
What Lessons Can Developing Countries Learn from China's Macroeconomic and Financial Approaches to Development?

Chapter 2: What Lessons Can Developing Countries Learn from China's Macroeconomic and Financial Approaches to Development?

2.1 Introduction and Context[10]

The Covid-19 crisis has highlighted the need for developing countries to preserve policy space in all of their binding agreements. This determines the extent to which countries effectively can use macroeconomic and other policy tools to increase government expenditures, impose temporary trade and capital account restrictions, relax banking and other rules, and innovate. With the advent of the crisis, on the monetary and financial policy fronts, many developing countries reduced interest rates, lowered banks' required reserve ratios (RRR), conducted rediscount operations, allocated subsided loans to targeted sectors and firms (e.g., agriculture, small and medium enterprises-SMEs), provided credit guarantees and gave debt moratorium for bank loans. Regarding the financial regulation front, many countries relaxed bank loan classification rules and those adopting the Basel III capital framework reduced the capital conservation buffers.

From the fiscal and income policies point of view, governments created fiscal packages to strengthen health sector responses, support businesses, and protect workers. Measures also included expanding unemployment benefits, broadening social protection coverage, transferring cash to the most vulnerable, setting price ceilings on essential food, and providing emergency food and shelter. In addition, authorities granted income and corporate tax exemptions and relief, including VAT (value-added tax) exemption and rebate measures and tax debt forgiveness. Concerning the external sector, import tariffs were lowered or temporarily exempted to specific products such as medical equipment and medicines, and some countries introduced current and capital account restrictions.

At the same time, major differences in responses could be noted among developing countries, including the scale of measures adopted and the number of instruments deployed. By the end of 2020, China and Indonesia had delivered relatively large monetary and fiscal packages: 4.7 and 4.3-8 per cent of GDP in Indonesia and China, respectively. In addition, these two countries had adopted a more comprehensive range of monetary, fiscal and tax instruments. China, for instance, deployed virtually all monetary policy instruments available to inject more liquidity into the financial system. Additionally, this country offered a fiscal subsidy of interest payment for targeted sectors, approved local government bonds issuance, and gave income and VAT exemption. However, the prolonged nature of the pandemic has made it imperative for developing countries to reassess their existing macroeconomic and financial policies.

[10] This chapter is prepared by Ricardo Gottschalk based on the papers undertaken by Feng, Li and Wu (2020), "The Macroeconomic Policy Framework for Structural Transformation: Experiences and Implications from China" available on https://unctad.org/system/files/official-document/BRI-Project_RP6_en.pdf.

Developing countries in all regions have been making efforts to meet the sustainable development goals (SDGs). To date, these efforts have not translated into an acceleration of growth and structural transformation, which are needed to meet these goals.

For the least developed countries (LDCs), the SDG 8 sets a target of seven per cent annual GDP growth for the 2016-2030 period. Yet, UNCTAD studies (2019a) show only 5 of 47 LDCs met this target in 2017, a decline from 15 countries at the beginning of the 2010s. Moreover, recent estimates similarly point to a small number of countries meeting this target from 2018 to 2020 and even fewer countries in 2021 (Traeger, 2020). An additional challenge is achieving even higher GDP growth rates, which is necessary for meeting several SDGs with environmental sustainability components. In other words, higher growth ought to be low-carbon growth to be consistent with what the Intergovernmental Panel on Climate Change proposes as "a minimally acceptable environmental target by 2030", which requires a strong shift to the generation of non-carbon energy.

Nevertheless, the fact is that GDP growth - be it low-carbon or not - is slowing down instead of accelerating. For developing countries, average annual growth rates were 6.3 per cent over the 2001-2008 period, then 4.8 per cent over 2009-2018 and are expected to be even lower in the coming years because of the Covid-19 effects. According to UNCTAD analysis, much of this declining trend is due to weak growth in the developed world, associated with austerity-centred macroeconomic policies. This weakness matters because developed economies constitute a major demand source for developing countries.

Fragile growth at the global level has been the case since the global financial crisis. In addition, since then, the world economy has been characterized by low trade dynamism and volatile commodity prices. The Covid-19 crisis has just reinforced these trends. Developing countries have initially responded by using the policy space they had accumulated during the commodity boom period of 2003-2008, but even so, economic growth gradually declined. Many countries are now witnessing high levels of external indebtedness and a situation of debt distress that further curbs future growth. Still, despite more challenging global circumstances and heightened policy constraints at the national level, developing countries can learn how to pursue rapid and sustained growth. This chapter focuses on possible lessons from China.

China's experience over the 1979-2018 period shows that rapid growth and structural transformation are possible and these twin goals can be sustained even when circumstances outside of the control of national authorities become challenging. The chapter argues that the key to China's experience is a macroeconomic policy framework that focuses on a growth strategy that is investment-led and is flexible enough to adapt to changing circumstances. Another lesson from China's 40 years of sustained growth is the role of public investment, not only at the early stages of development but also during the whole development process.

Unlike China, however, not many developing countries have the institutions, the market size, or the minimum absolute critical mass of human, technological and financial resources to support rapid and sustained transformation. So, while there are lessons to learn from China, they need to be selectively adopted and appropriately adapted. Additionally, the international context during which China experienced rapid expansion was characterized by a benign world trade environment. Although China has greatly benefited from this context, it has significantly changed. Notwithstanding, the fact is that China itself had to respond to major shocks and changing circumstances, including the East Asian crisis and the global financial crisis. It did so by showing extreme agility based on pragmatism, flexibility and gradualism.

This chapter will explore these elements in detail in section 2.2. Section 2.3 will discuss critical lessons from China's structural transformation, focusing on its approach, the tools it deployed, and the institutions it leveraged to achieve its long-term policy goals. Section 2.4 concludes and indicates the direction forward for developing countries achieving the SDGs and structural transformation.

2.2 China's Policies and Experiences

This section examines China's 40 years of development policy experience for rapid catch-up, growth, and transformation,[11] by focusing on China's ability to manage external shocks and mobilize resources for development. This section explores in detail which macroeconomic policy framework China had in place to achieve its development objectives. As mentioned in the previous section, three main elements stand out in analysing China's experience: pragmatism, flexibility and gradualism.

These three elements were deeply embedded in China's macro-policy framework through three vectors: i) proactive macroeconomic management, ii) financial reform and financial sector development, and iii) carefully managed capital account liberalization. With this framework, China's policymakers sought to achieve several policy objectives, including:

(a) *Mitigating macroeconomic fluctuations*. In a market-based economy operating through business cycles, macroeconomic fluctuations around a growth trend are common. In developing economies, these fluctuations are accentuated due to their structural characteristics. China's policy makers sought to be proactive in addressing this problem by attenuating such fluctuations to support growth through adoption of a range of counter-cyclical policy instruments, including fiscal and monetary policy tools, administrative orders and institutional reforms;

(b) *Supporting investment and exports*: growth had to be supported directly, not just indirectly, attenuating macro fluctuations. By fostering investment, through the deployment of fiscal and monetary policy tools (e.g., autonomous investment; low-

[11] This section summarizes the main points of two papers UNCTAD commissioned under its BRI project: the first on China's macroeconomic policy framework; the second on China's financial sector reforms. These papers were prepared under the leadership of Li Daokui and Zhao Changwen – see Feng et al. (2019) and Zhao et al (2019). They can be found on UNCTAD's website at: https://unctad.org/topic/south-south-cooperation/bri-platform.

interest rates) and by supporting exports through the adoption of a competitive exchange rate;

(c) *Maintaining financial stability*. China had in place a macro-prudential framework that emphasized, along the process of financial sector development, a financial system both dominated and denominated in local currency. The purpose was to reduce currency mismatches in the system, which could be a major source of financial instability. Policy makers also sought the objective of price stability but were not overly obsessed with stringent inflation targets, as they knew price shocks and price volatility tend to be more accentuated in developing economies and thus leeway is needed to deal with these price events;

(d) *Managing external shocks*. In an open, financialized world, volatile capital flows can be a primary source of shocks. Therefore, China sought to adopt a gradual approach to capital account liberalization, prioritizing first the liberalization of more stable flows, such as FDI, and only at a later stage liberalizing portfolio flows, known as more volatile;

(e) *Having in place an exchange rate regime that supported structural transformation*. Since having a competitive exchange rate was essential in China's policy framework, China authorities liberalized the exchange rate gradually, starting with a dual regime to give a competitive advantage to China's exporters, and only later moving to a unified exchange rate;

(f) *Tackling financial crises*. Protecting the economy from financial crises taking place elsewhere was essential. To this end, China accumulated large foreign reserves as a self-insurance mechanism; reserve accumulation was also the result of interventions in the foreign exchange markets to maintain a competitive exchange rate.

All these policy objectives were aimed at a growth-inducing macroeconomic environment. With such an environment in place, coupled with direct policy interventions to stimulate aggregate demand, China witnessed over the years a strong growth performance, fast export expansion, productive diversification, and a rapidly evolving growth-supporting financial system.

Regarding China's approach to financial sector development, China's authorities thought it was important to promote financial deepening for the following reasons: i) the seigniorage revenues it could generate; ii) the opportunities and instruments a deepened system could provide for residents to save; iii) the funds it could provide to support the expansion of productive capacity. China's authorities thought banking was better at earlier stages of development than capital markets for the following reasons: the banking sector requires less high skilled inputs and less complex institutional arrangements, is easier to regulate, and is less prone to crises. In practice, the emphasis on banking propelled the development of a credit economy, supporting the expansion of productive activities and rapid growth of employment, income, demand, profits, reinvestment, and savings.

Historically, China's banking sector evolved from mono-banking and then transformed into a multi-tier banking system. This process was embedded in an incentive mechanism termed the 'financial restraint model', which involves interest rate control, restricted entry of new financial institutions, and asset substitution restrictions. It was a model different from full financial liberalization that, by aiming for real positive interest rates (albeit below market rates) and creating renting opportunities, encouraged financial institutions to provide the required finance for the country's process of rapid industrialization. In addition, the banking system included development banks. The latter, known in China as policy banks, were needed to support above all infrastructure investment programs, which were a key driver of rapid catch up and transformation in China's case.

The prominent role that development banks played in China's development strategy was due to several factors. First, such banks did not operate in isolation but in articulation with the rest of the financial system. Second, they were well capitalized. Third, they had access to large, reliable sources of funding with the help of financial regulation. For instance, bonds issued by CDB faced zero per cent capital charges and status of good collateral by the central bank, thus becoming low-risk assets that other banks had an incentive to hold. Fourth, they were aligned with China's major national strategies by investing in priority sectors such as major infrastructures, regional development, upgrading traditional industries, and supporting strategic emerging industries. Finally, they did not take profits as a primary goal.

As mentioned earlier, an underlying characteristic of China's macroeconomic policy framework has been flexibility over time to support a rapidly growing economy undergoing significant structural changes. Apart from this flexibility, China' macroeconomic policy framework was coupled with pragmatism and gradualism, which was evident in many policies. One example is exchange rate management, in which levels of control changed in response to new circumstances and shocks. Another example is the liberalization of the balance of payments- particularly the financial account-, which was underscored by an experimentation process. The fiscal policy, which focuses on capital expenditure for capacity expansion and serves as a major counter-cyclical tool in crisis periods, also illustrates China's approach. Finally, the financial regulation is another case, once it has evolved to keep pace with a financial system growing rapidly in terms of size, depth, and complexity, and how the regulatory apparatus responded to such growth as well as to shocks. There was no rigid commitment to fixed rules, as these were adapted over time in response to new circumstances and needs. Reforms were gradual and pragmatic choices were made regarding the evolving roles of the state and the markets.

2.3 Key Lessons from China's Structural Transformation

Lessons from China for structural transformation in the macro and finance areas can be learned in terms of approach, tools, and institutions brought together for effective macroeconomic policy management.

Approach – In terms of approach, a key lesson from China's experience is that its macroeconomic framework was adaptable enough to respond to changing needs and circumstances. The framework imbued three key elements – pragmatism, flexibility and gradualism, all critical in China's development experience, and which can be essential for other developing countries as well for at least three reasons.

First, developing economies have been historically engaged in the global economy in a peripherical way, which requires flexibility to respond to business cycles taking place in the core of the economic system. Second, developing economies often have narrower economic structures, making them more susceptible to macroeconomic volatility and external shocks. This, again, requires flexibility, especially in terms of fiscal and monetary policy rules, and a cautious approach to trade and especially capital account liberalization. As China demonstrates, the latter should be carefully and gradually liberalized and managed with the help of control mechanisms that can be activated when needed to minimize major macroeconomic disturbances caused by excessive capital inflows or outflows.

Lastly, there is no fixed formula for a rapid catch up. Development is a process of trial and error and is part of it to experiment and change as an economy develops. Back in the 2000s, development economists, mainstream scholars, and international policy advisors, already stressed that these elements were important for countries to achieve the Millennium Development Goals (e.g., Cagatay et al., 2000; Gottschalk, 2005). For the future, these elements continue essential to the road towards the achievement of the SDGs.

Tools – Over time, public investment was among the tools that China consistently deployed. Public investment played a critical role in China's growth and transformation processes and can be vital for developing economies seeking to catch up with growth. Public investment can initiate a virtuous growth process, thus serving long-term and short-term objectives, such as a counter-cyclical tool to stimulate the economy in times of faltering demand.[12]

Currently, many developing countries facing low growth and thus in need of a growth driver find that private investment is not playing that role, even when the economy has a large private sector. Despite this situation, many international policy advisors recommend that governments fiercely seek an adequate business environment. The truth is that when domestic demand is weak and world trade- an alternative demand source- lacks traction, public investment is needed to crowd in private investment. In addition, public investment is a vital tool to help national governments to set expenditure priorities, and address social, environmental and economic needs as these arise or are anticipated as part of a long-term development strategy (Barbosa, 2020).

Related to the role of public investment, a broader element of an effective macroeconomic policy framework is public sector coordination, which can be found in China and other countries that achieved a rapid catch up growth and structural transformation in the last century. Public sector coordination is necessary to maximize gains. It is particularly important in the SDG context for two reasons: to explore synergies that may arise from the fact that various

[12] For an analysis of the role of public investment in growth, see inter alia McKinley (2008) and UNCTAD (2019b, Chapter 3).

SDGs are interrelated and to manage possible tensions that will also inevitably occur. Above all, public sector coordination, of which public investment is a key tool, is necessary to give a direction to growth in tender with national development objectives.

More public investment, however, requires fiscal policy space. Yet, such a space is hard to find when many developing countries are entering situations of debt distress, facing reduced ability to generate foreign exchange to sustain rapid growth in a context of weak global demand, and are blown off course now by the ongoing pandemic. The Chinese experience and other successful late industrializers show that part of the answer requires assessing fiscal space dynamically and not in a static way. Indeed, from a dynamic perspective, public investment plays a role in creating fiscal space by stimulating aggregate demand, growth, and tax revenue expansion which is a by-product of growth itself. In addition, public investment can be used to target bottlenecks, thereby creating new space for pro-growth policies.

Institutions – On the finance side, a key lesson from China is the financial institutions' role in supporting growth acceleration. Among all financial institutions, development banks are critical for expanding and diversifying productive capacity. Development banks supported the expansion of public and private enterprises, the urban sector development, the agricultural sector, the renovation of old industries, and now are focusing on China's shift towards green development. As highlighted above, these banks did not operate alone but with the support of the central bank and other financial institutions, which provided the large-scale funding needed to finance operations in multiple areas that were critical for transformative growth.

2.4 Conclusion and Way Forward for Developing Countries

When drawing up sustainable growth strategies, it is necessary to highlight that developing countries have distinct starting points and challenges. Adopting lessons from China, therefore, requires that policymakers take these realities into account. Moreover, the existing international environment differs from what China experienced during its development and transformation processes. These changing circumstances must be contemplated when designing a future strategy and its suitable macroeconomic framework.

Key emerging challenges facing developing countries include how to transition to a digital and green economy. Although China did not have to deal with these challenges during its 40 years of continuous development, China is facing them now. For developing countries, these challenges can also be seized as opportunities. For instance, the green challenge is a chance for developing countries to create an economy that is carbon neutral. Unlike developed economies, many developing countries do not have to phase out large fossil-fuel linked infrastructures or deal with stranded assets. In addition, a green transition can open the door for home-grown technologies and solutions, drawing on countries' strengths in specific areas and sectors. Concerning the digital economy, countries need to act strategically regarding how to engage in the digital era and, in particular, how to build a data economy while maintaining ownership and control over domestic data, which is a precious resource in the 21st century.

China is currently developing its own digital and green technologies. However, other developing countries should bear in mind that they do not have the advantages that China can count on in terms of market size or the ability to provide finance at a large scale. Against this backdrop, these countries can join forces and strengthen regional cooperation to overcome size barriers and other limitations. On finance, for instance, developing countries can enhance their regional development banks to finance regional digital and green infrastructures. As it is always important to recall, these banks are institutions that can design, execute and provide financing for complex, large-scale, and cross-border projects.[13]

A final message is that the same policy may yield different results in different countries due to their specific needs and circumstances. Therefore adapting China's policies to developing countries' ground realities is imperative; otherwise, the effectiveness of policies will be significantly diminished. In addition, and as argued above, policy implementation and adaptation imply that countries need to respond to dynamic situations.

[13] On the specific role of regional development banks in financing regional digital infrastructures, see Gottschalk (2019).

CHAPTER 3
A Self-discovery Journey: China's Industrial Policy Experience since 1978

Chapter 3: A Self-discovery Journey: China's Industrial Policy Experience since 1978

3.1 Industrialization: The Key Driving Force Behind China's Miracle[14]

One of the most prominent phenomena in modern economic history is China's rapid rise from a poor agrarian economy to global economic power. Since China embarked on its **"reform and opening-up"** journey in 1978, it has recorded four decades of 9.5% average annual GDP growth and lifted over 700 million people out of extreme poverty. In early 2021, China announced the eradication of extreme poverty based on its national poverty line.[15] Among various features and characteristics of such transformational growth, industrialization with technological advancement is probably the critical factor driving "China's economic miracle".

Some economic facts and figures clearly show that the industrial sector growth backs the economic rise of China. In absolute terms, as figure 1 demonstrates, China's Industry value-added (IVA) had surpassed the US and topped the global ranking since 2010, the same year when it became the second-largest economy in the world.

Figure 3.1: Industry value-added, selected regions, 1970–2017, (in current billion USD)

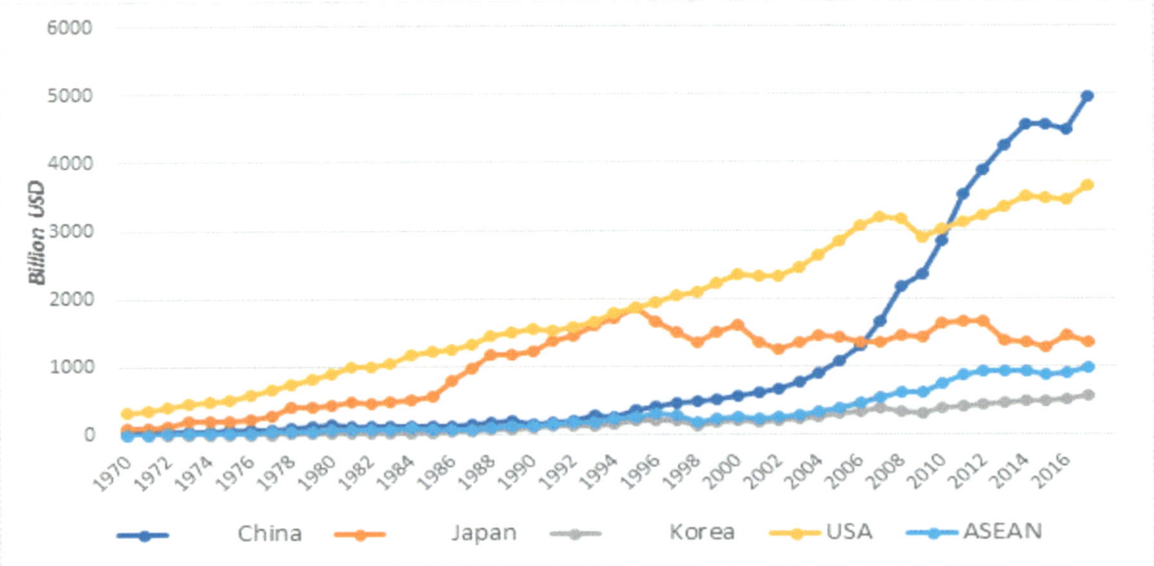

Source: UNCTADStat.

---

[14] This chapter is prepared by Dawei Wang. The author is grateful for the comments and insights from Richard Kozul-Wright on the earlier draft.

15 State Council Information Office of China: Poverty Alleviation: China's Experiences and Contribution http://english.www.gov.cn/archive/whitepaper/202104/06/content_WS606bc77ec6d0719374afc1b9.html (accessed on August 4th, 2021).

In terms of GDP component share, IVA was the most significant contributor to China's GDP component for most of the post-1978 period (Figure 3.2). [16] Another indicator of industrialization is the share of the industrial sector in total employment. As Figure 3.3 presents, such a share was about 17.3% in 1978, then increased to the peak of 30.3% in 2012.

Figure 3.2: Agriculture, industry, and services' contribution to GDP, China, 1970–2017, (percentage of total)

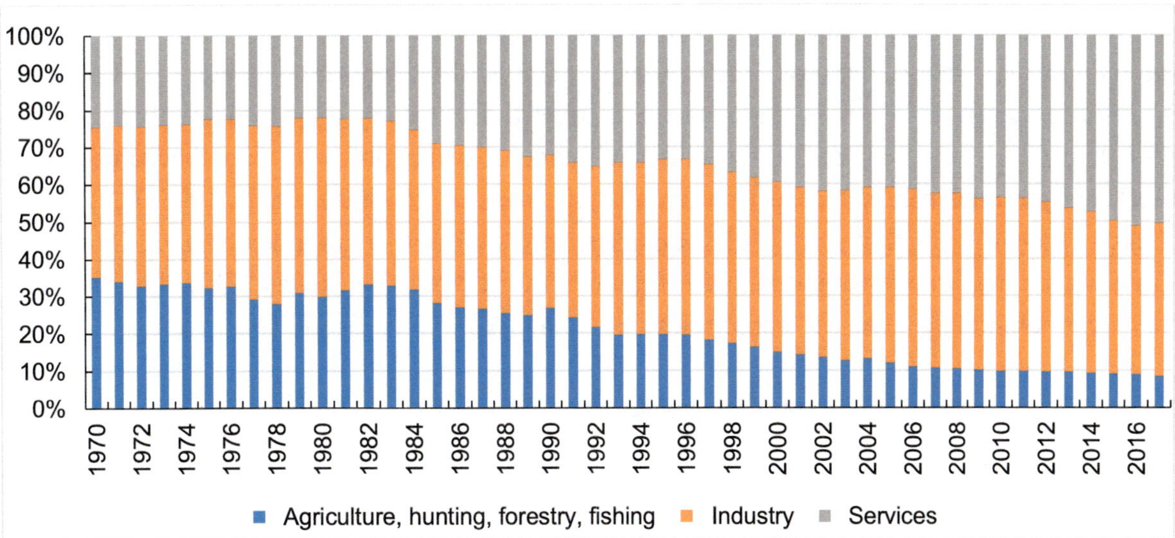

Source: UNCTADStat.

Figure 3.3: Share of secondary sector in total employment, China, 1978–2018

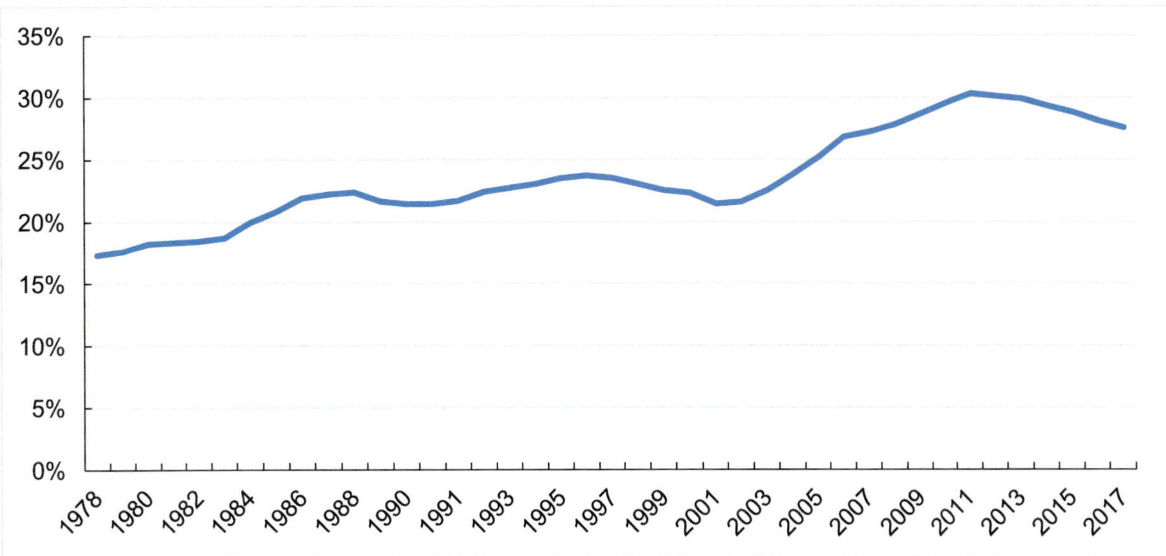

Source: Author's calculation based on the data from National Bureau of Statistics of China.

[16] According to UNCTADStat, since 2013, service sector has replaced the industry being the largest GDP component, but China's IVA/GDP ratio (41.3% in 2017) remains much higher than world average (25.4% in 2017).

Beyond comprehensive figures regarding the scale of industrial output or the share of the industrial sector in China's economy, the technological advancement of China's industrial sector is arguably even more impressive. One measurement would be labour productivity in industry, which is primarily driven by technological advancement in the industrial sector. Figure 3.4 shows the output as per unit of labour in China's secondary sector. The growth has also been very rapidly, increasing almost 67 times from 1978 to 2018. Another measurement would be economic complexity, which can be traced by the Economic Complexity Index (ECI) by the Harvard Development Lab.[17] Their data demonstrate that China has developed quite a sophisticated industrial sector which can be observed through the structure of its exports and ECI (Figure 3.3). China's export structure has been transformed enormously in the past decades. In 1979, over 50% of China's export revenue came from primary goods; today, that figure is less than 5%. Correspondently, the share of manufacturing products like mechanical and electrical products has increased significantly. In terms of ECI ranking, in 1995, China was ranked at the 46th position among 133 countries, corresponding to an index of 0.32. China has gradually climbed the rank, and in 2019 it stood at the 16th position (index 1.35), though it still lags a bit behind key advanced economies like Japan (No.1) and the US (No.12).[18]

Figure 3.4: Labour productivity in the secondary sector (index number 1=1978), China, 1978–2018

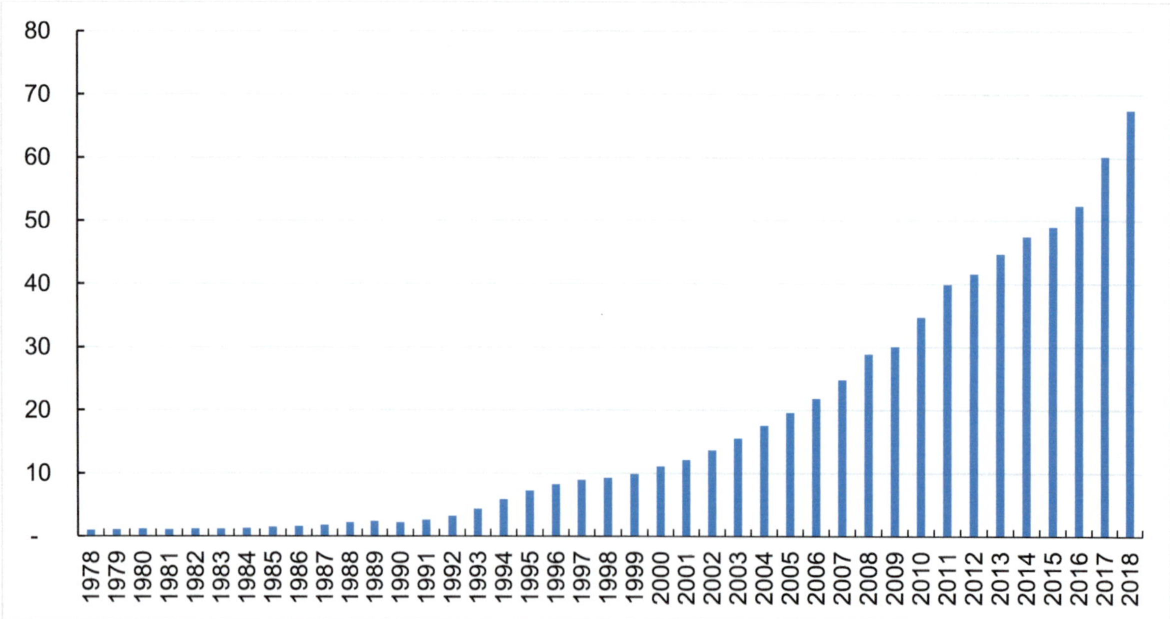

Source: author's calculation based on the data of National Bureau of Statistics of China.

[17] Economic complexity is used to describe the knowledge intensity of an economy. Learning or improving productive knowledge requires structural change. Economic complexity, therefore, is expressed in the composition of an economy's productive output and reflects the structures that emerge to hold and combine knowledge. The detailed definition and mathematical methods of calculating ECI can be found in Hausmann, Hidalgo et.al (2011) https://growthlab.cid.harvard.edu/files/growthlab/files/harvardmit_atlasofeconomiccomplexity.pdf.(accessed on August 4th, 2021).

[18] The Atlas of Complexity Rankings https://atlas.cid.harvard.edu/rankings (accessed on August 4th, 2021).

Figure 3.5: Gross exports measured by Economic Complexity Index, China, 2019

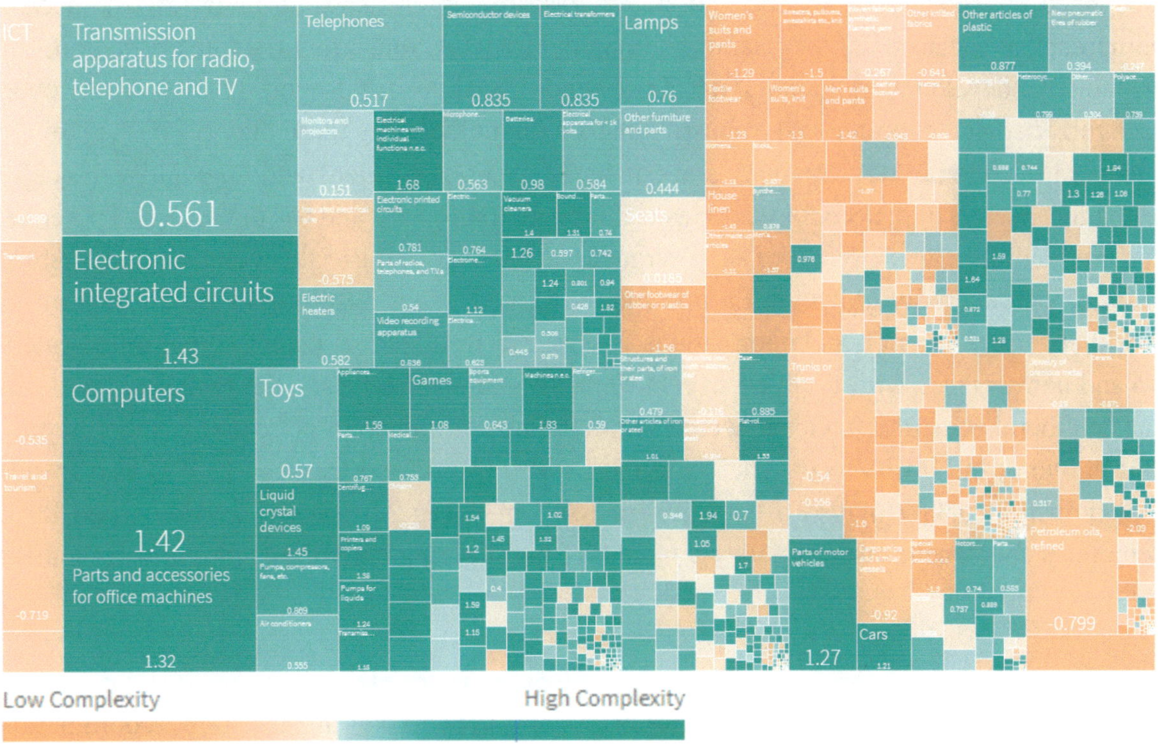

Source: Harvard CID.

The development of a strong manufacturing industry capability has driven economic diversification and improved economic resilience. During the recent global efforts to combat the Covid-19 pandemic, protective and medical supplies like masks and ventilators became essential and urgent. With a massive and rapid resource mobilization, within just one month-February 2020- China's daily production of masks increased 11 times, reaching 116 million pieces per day. *Wuling*, a Chinese automobile manufacturer, spent only 76 hours to produce its first automatic mask machine from scratch.[19] With covid-19 cases under control in China but spreading globally, China became the major global exporter of productive supplies, exporting about 3.86 billion pieces of masks just from March and early April 2020, according to China's Customs Administration.

There is little doubt on the significance of industrialization to development. Both academics and policymakers increased interest in exploring this topic in recent years. In terms of global policy consensus, the UN 2030 Agenda adopted in 2015 has flagged the bold ambition to eradicate poverty, leave no one behind, and guarantee a habitable planet. Notably, in a set of goals and targets towards transformative sustainable development, promoting inclusive and sustainable industrialization and raising the industry's share of employment and GDP were identified as essential targets.

---

[19] Xinhua news agency report, http://www.xinhuanet.com/auto/2020-03/07/c_1125677242.htm (accessed on April 9th, 2020).

Such renewed interest in the role of industrialization and industrial policy to development has also been reflected in academic and policy research interests. UNCTAD (2016) made a comprehensive analysis of the relations among industrialization, structural transformation, and sustainable development in its 2016 Trade and Development Report (TDR). This report recognized that "a broad and robust domestic manufacturing base has been the key to successful economic development, since it helps generate virtuous and cumulative linkages with other sectors of the economy, drives technological progress, and has the strongest potential for productivity gains". Rodrik (2016) argued, "it was the industrial revolution that enabled sustained productivity growth in Europe and the United States, resulting in the division of the world economy into rich and poor nations. It was industrialization again that permitted catch-up and convergence with the West of non-Western nations. For years, the IMF has advocated for neoliberal economic policies, which views the use of industrial policy as a "taboo topic". But in one of the IMF's recent staff working papers, Cherif and Hasanov (2019) also argued that industrial policy played a "preeminent role" in Asian Miracles. They identified three principles for "true industrial policy", including highlighting state intervention to fix market failures.

However, economic history shows that industrialization is not easy to achieve. It is particularly challenging for later developing countries once domestic (market imperfections, coordination failure.) and international constraints (Dutch disease, for example) can impede their efforts. Hence, overcoming those binding constraints might require a "big push" from the state through a well-designed and functional strategy: industrial policy. That will bring us to a long-contested issue: the role and the effectiveness of industrial policy in economic development.

As Ha-Joon Chang (2002) observed in his book, *Kicking Away the Ladder*, ITT (industrial, trade and technology) policies have stood at the center of controversies in the theory of economic development for a few hundred years. After examining the economic policies in various countries, he demonstrated that, since Britain's Industry Revolution, state policy intervention had been widely used by today's advanced economies in Europe and North America and the newly industrialized economy (NIE) in east Asia. Yet, the question is that industrial policy can be a double-edged sword. Like many other economic policy tools, industrial policy can also bring inefficient investment, rent-seeking, among other detrimental effects to development. So how to design, implement, and update industrial policy is the key. That is precisely the theme of this chapter.

This chapter explores the evolution of China's industrial policies in section 3.2, which has been proven generally successful judging from the industrialization outcome. Section 3.3 draws learning experiences from the policy evolution, which could help enrich the understanding of the industrial policy role. Section 3.4 concludes and provides a way forward as recommendations for other developing countries.

3.2 China's Industrialization and Industrial Policy Since 1978

Many factors have contributed to China's industrialization: abundant land resources, low-cost and competent human capital, participation in global value chains, among other factors. But it has been widely noted that well-designed and effectively implemented industrial policy and strong state capability has played a vital role in this process. China was viewed as the "most dedicated practitioner" in using the industrial policy approach to "accelerate, widen and deepen their industrialization paths". (UNCTAD, 2016)

(a) Brief Story Before 1978

China embarked on its "***reforming and opening-up***" journey in 1978. However, its industrialization efforts could be traced back to the early 1950s, shortly after the establishment of the People's Republic of China in 1949, when it was a poor and traditional agricultural economy.

Starting from 1950, China implemented a quite comprehensive industrialization programme, later called ***156 Projects***. With the technical and human resources, machinery and equipment, and concessional loan support from the Soviet Union, China built about 150 major heavy industry projects, which have been considered solid foundations of China's industrialization. In 1952, China's IVA had only a small share (17.6%) of its GDP.[20] But with very rapid growth, the industry sector became the largest contributor to the GDP in 1959. In 1960, this ratio even reached a high level of 39.1%.

However, the Chinese industrialization was negatively impacted when the Sino-Soviet relations were disrupted, causing the sudden and premature completion of the *156 Projects,* and the economic Great Leap strategy failed in 1960. The IVA/GDP ratio dropped sharply in 1961 (29.8%). It was not until 1970 that the IVA again surpassed the agriculture value-added, becoming the largest contributor to GDP growth. Despite its large scale, China's industry was overly dependent on low-level technology. Its structure was largely biased to heavy industry, making its manufacturing products uncompetitive on international markets and unable to meet domestic consumer demand. Such status reflected the Chinese trade structure: in the late 1970s and early 1980s, primary products accounted for over 50% of export revenue. While in 2018, the value of primary commodities was just 5% of China's export, manufacturing products accounting for 95%.[21]

Since 1978, China's industrialization has progressed very fast and its economic policies, including industrial policy, have also been iterated rapidly. To elaborate the story as clearly as possible, we will trace the policy evolution by dividing the four decades (1978-2018) into three phases: 1978-2001, 2002-2008 and 2009-2019. We identify 2001 and 2008 as two milestones

---

[20] The IVA data is from China National Bureau of Statistics, unless stated otherwise.

[21] The share of primary commodities in total export value was 50.3% in 1980, and 5.4% in 2018, according to the data of National Statistics Bureau.

because of the WTO ascension and the Global Financial Crisis, which significantly impacted China's growth and supporting policies.

(b) Phase I: 1978-2001

Within the 23 years that separate the Chinese "reform and opening up" journey and its accession to the WTO, China's IVA increased from RMB 0.16 trillion to RMB 4.39 trillion. The increase in the industry value-added was accompanied by technological upgrading and structural change.

Like other developing countries, in 1978, the most challenging problem for China's economic development- including the industry sector- was finance and technology. At that time, the national foreign exchange reserve was just 167 million USD. The technology level and the industry's productivity were far behind industrialized economies. A well-known story about the study visit of a high-level government delegation to Europe in 1978 illustrates this point: the delegation, headed by then Vice-premier Gu Mu, was stunned by the vast technology and productivity gap between China and European countries. During a visit to a German coal mining, it was noticed that the productivity of a German worker was about 80 times higher than its Chinese counterparts. Once in Beijing, the delegation prepared the *Report on The Visit to Five Countries of Western Europe*, and also made an 8-hour oral briefing to China's leadership, including Deng Xiaoping. The report proposed a set of policy recommendations including expanding trade, advancing science and technology, utilizing foreign capital and technology to develop manufacturing sector, and reforming economic governance system (Gu, 1978) which was widely considered to impact the formulation of China's catch-up strategy characterized by a set of integrated industrial-trade-finance-FDI policies.

From the early 1980s to the mid-1990s, China began to use foreign capital (including loans and FDI) to mitigate its financial constraints. From 1979 to 1991, total loan inflows to China (both from official and commercial creditors) accounted for 52.5 billion USD, while total FDI stock amounted to 25.6 billion USD.[22] Beyond overcoming finance constraints, China particularly welcomed capital inflows to upgrade its technology levels. On the one hand, with capital inflows, China had a stronger purchasing power for importing advanced equipment and technology. Although available data for this period varies, Luan (2006) shows that, from 1980 to 1989, China imported 20.9 billion USD on equipment and technology. According to MOFCOM's official historical review, within three years (1983-1985), China spent about 3 billion USD implementing a plan named "3000 projects" aimed at upgrading enterprises projects. On the other hand, China started to explore how to upgrade its technology level through FDI (mainly in joint venture mode in the 1980s). For instance, during a technology transfer negotiation in 1978, General Motors proposed to China's leadership establishing a

---

[22] According to Liu Jianli, 70 Years History of China's FDI Inflow: Pathway, Effectiveness, and Experience, from Ministry of Commerce official website http://chinawto.mofcom.gov.cn/article/ap/p/201912/20191202923754.shtml (accessed on January 25, 2022).

joint venture.[23]The proposal was approved by Deng Xiaoping, as he believed it was practical to overcome the financial and technological constraints. [24]Meanwhile, before joining the WTO, China also used various Trade-Related Investment Measures (TRIMs), including local content requirements and export performance, to protect its enfant industry when opening to FDI.

At the same time and assisted by the inflow of capital and technology, China put structural adjustment at the centre of its industrial policy by mobilizing resources to develop the industry in tradable sectors. China firstly put light industry, particularly the textile industry, as the priority. In 1980, the country adopted a policy called "six-priorities", which through government planning directed more productive resources- like finance, power, transportation, and technology - to the textile industry. But such structure adjustment was not seen in static terms. China continued to employ policy support to adjust its industry structure to fit the evolving circumstance. In the mid-1980s, when the government believed the "concerted development among agriculture, light industry and heavy industry was progressed", China shifted the priority towards "fundamental industry", which mainly referred to the infrastructure (including power generation and transportation facilities), electronics, and machinery sectors. The rationale was that such a fundamental industry could lay a solid foundation for further upgrading of its overall industry sectors (Wei, 2021).

Technology upgrading and industry adjustment improved the position of China in international trade. China's total import and export value, which was about 20 billion USD in 1978, reached100 billion just ten years later. Its export structure also changed: as already mentioned, over 50% of China's export was primary goods, while in 1991, manufacturing products accounted for 77.5% of its exports. It further led to the trade balance improvement. In most years of the 1980s and early 1990s, China ran a moderate trade deficit, but since the mid-1990s, it has become a significant merchandise exporter and surplus country.

Given the evolving situation, China updated its policy portfolio after the mid-1990s. In 1995, China introduced a new policy measure in its FDI policy: catalogue management. In the two policy documents, ***"Temporary Direction Guidelines for FDI"*** and ***"Industry Guidance Catalogue of FDI"***, the government categorized FDI projects into five types: *encouraging*, *limiting A*, *limiting B*, *prohibiting*, and *allowing.* Furthermore, the government provided preferential treatment to *encouraging* and *limiting B* types- mostly manufacturing projects- to facilitate its manufacturing industry development.

In parallel with the FDI policy change, China's industrial policy became more mature in the 1990s. In 1994, China adopted the first comprehensive policy guidance for industry development: the Industrial ***Policy Outline for the 1990s*** (IPO 1990).[25] The IPO 1990 aimed at upgrating the country industrial instructure and elaborated four major pillars for China's industrial policy framework: the

---

[25] The original text of the IPO 1990s can be found in official site of China's central government: http://www.gov.cn/gongbao/shuju/1994/gwyb199412.pdf (accessed on April 3rd, 2020).

industry's structure, organization, technology, and spatial distribution. It also identified the principles, decision-making procedures, review mechanisms, and government agencies' roles in the industrial policymaking process. About the development priorities, the IPO 1990 highlighted as fundamental industries (including infrastructure), high-tech, machinery and electronics, petrochemical, automobile manufacturing, and construction industries.

In the 1990s, besides the technology introduced from advanced countries, China accelerated the strengthening of national R&D capabilities. In order to advance the domestic industry's technological level, the government began to use multiple policy measures, including setting government long-term technology development plans, investing in fundamental science research, encouraging commercializing R&D outcomes, and establishing high-tech industrial parks. In the late 1990s and early 2000s, the government prioritized information, bio-engineering, new energy, material and environmental industries. For advancing technology level, China also encouraged the restructuring of large enterprises, most state-owned ones (SOEs), not only in Phase I but also in Phase II and III.

In 1997, China started a three-years plan on SOE reform,[26] further progressing the strategy of "grasping the large and letting go of the small", which was the theme of SOE reform since the early 1990s. In the following years, many small SOEs were privatized: while 24% of firms in the 1990s were SOEs, this ratio dropped to 10% in 2005, and to 3% in 2014 (Wei et al. 2016). But on the other hand, large SOEs have been consolidated through rounds of restructuring and merging. The scale and competitiveness of major SOEs have therefore been improved. In 1997, only three Chinese enterprises (all SOEs) were included in Fortune 500, while in 2019, there were 129 Chinese firms in that list, and 88 of them were SOEs. Meanwhile, with the increased number of large and medium-sized enterprises (including SOEs and private-owned) emerging in China, their R&D rose sharply, as figure 3.6 shows.

Figure 3.6: R&D expenditure of large and medium-sized enterprises, China, 1997–2018, (Billion RMB)

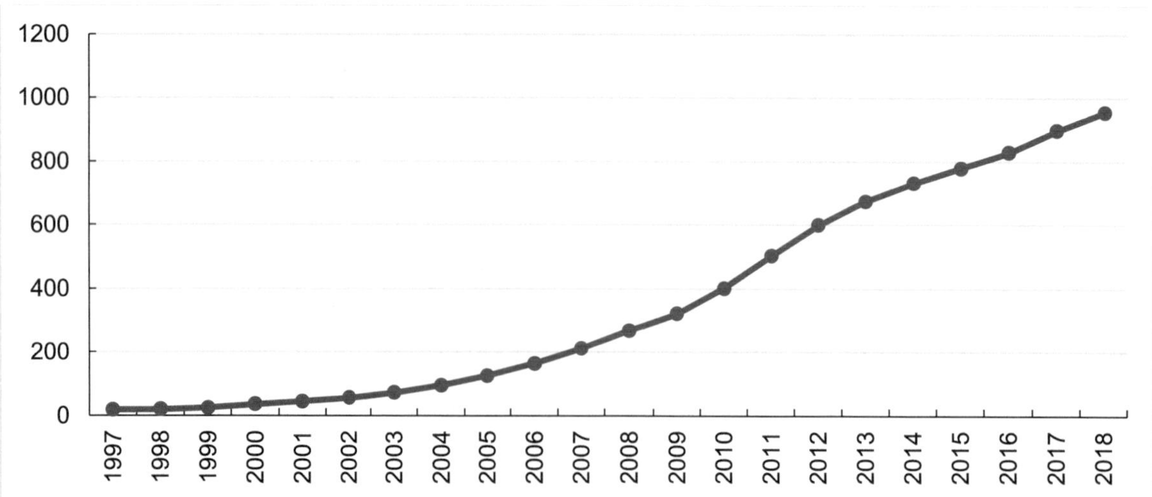

Source: National Bureau of Statistics of China.

[26] It actually has gone further beyond 3 years.

(c) Phase II: 2002-2008

China's accession to the WTO is a milestone event in the country's development path. The WTO accession deepened the country's integration into the global economy. It is associated with improved and more predictable global market access and reduced domestic space to shape its economic policy.

In terms of policy space, before its accession, China had substantially revised its economic policy and law system to be compatible with the WTO rules system. After the accession, apart from lowering import tariff, China was also restricted in using some previous applicable industrial policy measures, including industry protective measures, trade-related investment measures (TRIMs), export subsidies, to mention a few restrictions. But the WTO accession did not prohibit China from using policy rules within its allowed space. So, China updated its industrial policy measures accordingly. Zhao (2012) summarized several changing aspects of China's industrial policy after WTO accession, including changes from the supply side to the demand side, from emphasizing long-term objective to short-term objective, increasing environmental perspectives, focusing more on systemic policies, and adopting rules more consistent with international patterns, among other modifications.

In terms of actual measures, China's updated industrial policies are mainly reflected in the following three sets of policy portfolio measures.

The first was a further adjustment in the industrial structure. From 2002, China proposed a new policy called "***New Industrialization Path***" (NIP) as the guiding principle in forming its industrial policy. The NIP encourages the adoption of information technology to advance industrialization by improving technology level, resource efficiency, and corporate profit (Wei, 2021). Based on this principle, China prioritized developing high-tech, fundamental, advanced manufacturing and equipment manufacturing industries in its ongoing industry structure adjustment after 2001.

The second was fostering sustainable development. After more than two decades of rapid industrialization and urbanization, China was facing rising pressure of environmental degradation. Since the Ninth Five Years Plan period (1996-2000), China had already introduced an ecological dimension into its industrial strategy, notably regarding the energy industry development.[27] However, the challenge has worsened in the early 2000s, especially for air and water pollution, as reported by the Chinese government in its annual ***China's Environment Status Report***.[28] Therefore, the sustainable development element was highlighted more in its industrial policy as observed in NIP and several follow-up policies

---

[27] The Ninth Five Year Plan and Visionary Goals Outline for 2010, http://www.npc.gov.cn/wxzl/gongbao/2001-01/02/content_5003506.htm (accessed on April 9th, 2020).

[28] China's Ministry of Ecology and Environment http://www.mee.gov.cn/gkml/sthjbgw/qt/200910/W020091031558582294247.pdf (accessed on August 3rd, 2021).

documents. These policies were intended to promote a cleaner development, including through structure adjustment and even closing some highly polluting enterprises.

The third set of policies was the continuous updating of policy toolkits. About two years after its WTO accession, China declared further progress on market-oriented economic reforms, allowing market forces to play a "fundamental role" in resource allocation. But China always tried to build a sophisticated balance between the role of markets and state policy intervention. For example, in 2004, China reformed its investment management system. On the one hand, the government didn't require the enterprise to submit its investment project plan for approval unless government funding was involved. On the other hand, the government introduced a catalogue management method. For several investments and industry structure adjustments, the government developed a catalogue developed from 2002 to 2005. This scheme was probably replicated from the FDI guidance catalogue, and investments were categorized into three kinds: *encouraging, limiting and eliminating.* The government provided some concessional conditions- like finance and land - for "encouraging" investments and prohibited enterprises from investing in the "eliminating" category.

(d) Phase III: 2009-2019

In the early 2000s, China registered the best performance period in terms of GDP growth and industrialization. From 2002 to 2011, China's annual GDP growth rate maintained a level above 9%. Within just one decade, the Chinese GDP and IVA increased over fourfold, reaching RMB 48.8 trillion and 19.5 trillion respectively. As a result, in 2010, China overtook Japan's position and became the world's second-largest economy. In the same year, China also surpassed the US as the largest manufacturing economy. But since 2012, its growth rate has declined to around 7% or 6%. In the first quarter of 2020, mainly due to the Covid-19 locking down policy, China even registered a negative growth rate of 6.8%. But with the rebound of production and export in the second half-year, China eventually reached a positive growth rate of 2.3% in 2020.

Two major factors might have caused China's slower growth rate during Phase III. The first one is related to an external factor, namely a sluggish global trade that followed the Global Financial Crisis (GFC). In 2009, global merchandise exports registered a sharp decline (-12%), posing a severe challenge to China's economy given the high dependency on export (31% of its GDP in 2008). Its merchandise export declined by 18.3% in 2009. As China injected a massive fiscal stimulus plan, known as the ***4 Trillion Plan***, its GDP growth remained relatively high. However, its growth decreased significantly after 2011, though still high compared with other economies. Meanwhile, other challenges like the industry's overcapacity, heavy pollution, and inadequate innovation remain unsolved.

Against this backdrop, China has adjusted its industrial policy to adapt to the changing environment during that period. From 2008 to 2011, the policy focused on safeguarding growth to offset the GFC shock. With the ***4 Trillion Plan,*** China heavily invested in infrastructure building. Furthermore, since early 2009, China implemented an ***Industry***

Rejuvenation Plan (IRP) covering ten systemic sectors: automobile, steel, ship building, petrochemical, light industry, textile, non-ferrous metal, equipment manufacturing, electronic information, and modern logistics. Investment in infrastructure and IRP played an essential role in maintaining a relatively high growth rate after the GFC and shaping the economic policy formulation after this period.

Regarding industrial policy, the role of STI (Science, Technology and Innovation) was placed at the core, particularly the aspect of innovation. Liu & Sun (2007) studied 289 innovation policy cases that China formulated in the period of 1980-2005 and found China increasingly strengthened the coordination between STI and economic policies. However, despite of rapid growth and technology advancement for several decades, the Chinese government also realized that China still faces a huge technology gap with developed countries, which makes the country's key industrial technology heavily dependent on other countries. Therefore, China adopted ***National Mid- and Long Term Science and Technology Development Planning Outline (2006-2010)***, aiming to promote "self-dependent innovation" (Hu, 2006).

In 2015, China's State Council adopted an industrial plan called ***Made in China 2025***, which selected ten advanced technology and equipment areas encompassing information technology, robot and high-end equipment manufacturing, space and aviation, advanced transportation system and new materials, to mention the key areas. In the subsequent period, China has particularly encouraged applying digital technology to upgrade its industry. In 2015, to seize the opportunity of information and digital technology revolution, the government also adopted the ***Internet Plus Action Plan,*** which required the deep integration of Internet innovations with economic and social sectors to foster new driving forces of economic growth. (He & Sun, 2020). Later in 2019 and 2020, it identified additional seven "***new infrastructures,***" including 5G, UHV, high-speed rail transportation, data centre, artificial intelligence, NEV charging pile, and internet.

Clearly, in the post GFC period, China used industrial policy tools very frequently to address various growth challenges and it has generally worked quite well. Furthermore, Zhao (2012) and Jiang and Li (2018) suggest that, due to policymakers' experience accumulated throughout the years and their capacity development, the government's policy toolkit has become more diverse and mature. Economic policy measures like fiscal instruments, credit policy, standard-setting, pricing mechanism, catalogue management, regional development plan, and industrial park plan have been often used, rather than solely relying on administrative measures. Meanwhile, although the government continues its dominant role in industrial policy formulation, the decision-making procedure has become more open and transparent, allowing other actors like enterprise, experts, and the general public to voice their opinion in the policy-making process.

3.3 Learnings from China's Industrial Policy

(a) Why Do Developing Countries Need an Industrial Policy?

Before delving into detailed experiences and lessons from China's industrial policy, it is necessary to discuss the role and the impact of industrial policy in promoting economic development in a general sense.

As resource allocation across sectors matters for economic growth, misallocation partly explains the productivity variance among countries, which may cause the income gap among countries. Hence, structural transformation, pushing factors like labour and capital from low productivity sectors- like traditional agriculture- to modern high productivity sectors- like manufacturing-, has always been the key for catch-up and sustained economic growth. This structural transformation, while inextricably associated with industrialization, could also lead to a narrower income gap among countries.

However, as many previous pieces of research have observed, such structural transformation or industrialization process could be subject to two kinds of binding constraints: government and market failures. Regarding government failure, Rodrik (2008) shows that specific policy reforms that target improving institutions that may involve property rights or contract enforceability and others could be helpful to relax binding growth constraints. Concerning market failures, many authors have found that market imperfection -including the existence of learning and coordination externalities- fundamentally impede developing countries from completing their transformation mission (Matsuyama 1992, Hausmann and Rodrik 2003, McMillan and Rodrik 2011). In an open economy situation, the so-called "Dutch Disease" may also negatively impact the transformation in developing countries.[29] Therefore, overcoming those binding constraints justifies that developing countries maintain policy space during integration and develop targeted and effective industrial policies to provide a "big push" to address the market failures to reach industrialization targets.

With reference to China's experience in terms of industrial policy, after assessing the overview on the evolution of its policy in the past decade, we may find that those policies were well targeted in addressing both government and market failures and aimed to relax the binding constraints.

(b) General Experience of China's Economic Policy

Since 1978, China has put tremendous efforts into exploring the appropriate economic policies that could push the country to achieve its growth and development goals. The adopted policies have been proven effective and quite successful. Although China's policies may differ across sectors or regions, experimentation and pragmatism are two key "common features" evident in

[29] In an open economy, the tradable but traditional sector (like agriculture or other primary goods for many developing countries) could gain from increased world price. But such gains may cause the appreciation of its currency, increased demand for its non-tradable sector and biased factor allocation favoring traditional sector, which all could impede the development of its modern sector.

various policies. In the 1980s, former Chinese leader Deng Xiaoping made two broadly known metaphors to explain these two basic logics in policy formulation.

The first is "*crossing the river by groping for the stones*". When the "reform and opening-up" process began, China was unique in terms of its national circumstance if compared with other countries. There's not much ready and applicable experience for it to follow, even though Japan's growth and policy experiences provided some reference and learning in the 1980s. Therefore, China had to keep testing policy options to select the most effective ones. For example, in the earlier 1980s, inward FDI mostly flooded to higher return "non-productive" sectors such as luxury hotels or other kinds of leisure facilities, which would not serve the objective of advancing technology and industrialization. Since 2007, in line with environmental protection and sustainable development aims, China has encouraged FDI in greener and cleaner sectors like renewable energy while restricted or prohibited the "heavy-polluting" and "highly energy-wasting" projects. Hence, China kept testing methods to guide FDI and finally developed a catalogue management method that has proven quite effective.

A more recent example is the policy promoting "smart manufacturing", launched by China's Ministry of Industrialization and Information Technology (MIIT) in 2015. Every year, MIIT identified pilot projects and provided policy support (like funding R&D) to test the effectiveness of supporting policy, then gradually expanded the pilot programme. From 2015 to 2018, it increased the pilot projects from 46 to 99 projects.

The second metaphor is: "*It doesn't matter whether it is a white cat or a black cat, as long as it catches mice, it is a good cat*". Development thinking in the past decade has always been involved in various political and strategic debates, like state and market, integration, policy space, among other topics. For China, such a "philosophical" debate was even more sensitive as it could involve political and legal system debates. Deng's metaphor rejected any "prescription" or "panacea" regardless of its origin but focused on actual policy effectiveness when designing and evaluating development policies. That also explained why China's approach has always been highly time and location specific. China has gradually integrated in the world economy and explored global market opportunities. Nonetheless, China was very cautious in capital account liberalization and retained policy space to support the industrialization process, which differs from the typical neoliberal ideas of simply leaving the process to the market and private entrepreneurs.

(c) Specific Experience of China's Industrial Policy

On top of those general policy philosophies or rules, we may find out some interesting learning experience from China's industrial policy through revisiting its policy evolution.

- **Setting High-Level Ambition**

In their working paper about industrial policy, Cherif & Hasanov (2019) argued that "the state has to set the level of ambition of its goal and then implement the right policies while imposing accountability and being able to adapt fast as conditions change". China's experience in advancing its industrialization may provide a perfect deliberation of this argument.

Even in the early 1950s, when China was still a traditional agricultural economy and was building trade relations with the rest of the world, the country's leadership realized that external trade should serve the purpose of expanding industrial production.[30] Another example was about China's FDI policy: in the early 1980s, most of the inward FDI flooded into projects like luxury hotels, wine production, which China considers as belonging to the "non-productive" sectors. For this reason, since 1986, the government decided to use policy guidance to encourage FDI flow into "productive" sectors, like energy, transportation infrastructure, advanced technology industry, among other areas.

- **Focus A: Structure Adjustment**

As already mentioned, many studies in developmental economics have established strong causal relations among factor allocation, structural transformation, productivity, and development. Beyond the factor allocation among sectors- for instance, from agriculture to manufacturing - an allocation within sectors also matters for industrialization.

One of the constant and key themes of China's industrial policy is structure adjustment. In the early 1980s, the government pushed investment towards the light industry, mainly textile. Then in the later 1980s, fundamental industries such as energy and transportation became the focus as they could support industry development across the board. In the 1990s, the government started targeting both infrastructure and high-tech industries, proposing the concept of pillar industry and strategic industry reconfiguration. Since 2001, China has put high-tech, information, equipment manufacturing, renewable energy and other "strategic emerging" industries at the core. Even though the focus of the industrial policy keeps changing, it follows a persistent principle: pushing the factor towards the sector that will generate the highest possible productivity and return. These measures are not simply defined as short-term profitability but more widely as trade revenues or other social-economic effects.

- **Focus B: Technology Advancement**

The significance of technology advancement to economic growth and development cannot be overemphasized and China attaches great importance to this in its policy strategy. Former Chinese national leader Deng Xiaoping has once described the role of science and technology as "the first productivity". Therefore, in China's industrial policy, technological upgrading has always been prioritized together with structural adjustment.

---

[30] Su Ling, Strategic Decision and Basic Experience of Foreign Trade at the Early Stage of New China, http://dangshi.people.com.cn/n/2014/0504/c384616-24971826-2.html accessed Feb.10 of 2022.

Despite the changing strategy for technological upgrading, two basic logic principles can be recognized. The first one is improving domestic institutions. As documented by Cao and Yuan (2019), China has issued 20 national-level policies, regulations and laws concerning advancing STI since 1978. At least half of those policy documents and legislations aimed to build a patent protection system and safeguard incentives for scientific researchers' work, strengthening institutions as China's patent and IPR protection system was relatively weak before 1978.

The second principle is constantly pushing for upgrading the industry's technological level. In the 1980s, more efforts were put in importing advanced machinery equipment and "applicable technology". In the 1990s, Science and Education for National Invigoration was initiated to reinforce national capacity in R&D. Then, in the 2000s, the strategy shifted to self-innovation. Along with the changing focus of the strategy, China also keeps updating its policy tools, including equipment import, technology transfer, government investment in R&D, high-tech park, catalogue management, and talent strategy, which composes a quite effective STI system.

- **Integrated Policy System**

Industrialization is both the means and the end of structural transformation, which is essential to reach sustainable development. It is not just about building factories but also the result of a multidimensional development that involves finance, technology, human capital, institutions, and productivity. This process, therefore, requires an integrated and mutually reinforcing policy intervention, which is another key learning of China's industrialization experience. This chapter focuses on industrial policy, but it might not work well without a whole set of development policies in trade, FDI, education, STI, employment, and urbanization. In combination, these policies have contributed to forming a virtuous circle and jointly pushed a rapid and a pretty successful industrialization.

An example in this regard is the trade and industrial policies.[31] As mentioned, in the early 1980s, China prioritized the development of the textile industry. One of the reasons for doing so was the global competitiveness of China's textile goods. According to a People's Daily editorial *Accelerating the Development Is Necessary for Economic Adjustment* on 23rd January 1981, about 45% of foreign exchange revenue of China's export came from the textile industry. With the accumulation of foreign exchange reserves, China could purchase more advanced technologies and equipment to reinvest in its industrial development and further promote structure adjustment on power generation, transportation infrastructure, R&D, and high-tech industries. With industrialization and technological advancement, China has diversified its economy and strengthened its position in international trade, becoming the leading global manufacturing exporter. In a nutshell, China's successful economic development story results from a set of integrated policies in various economic areas, which industrial policy is situated at the core and has been reinforced with other policies.

[31] The chapter on GVCs provides more specific analysis on this topic.

- **"Walking on Two Legs"**

When Chinese national leaders explain their policy formulation, "walking on two legs" is also a frequently quoted metaphor even since the later 1950s. This metaphor refers to the importance of maintaining a dynamic balance among multiple policy options, and it is also helpful in explaining the logic of China's industrial policy, specifically on two aspects:

The first "leg" refers to integration and policy space. China's development and industrialization are highly dependent on global markets, particularly since 2001, with the trade to GDP ratio beating a record of 67% in 2006. But China has also maintained policy space to use policy tools to promote industrialization. This balance has been well described in the self-explanatory principle in China's economic policy since the mid-1990s that is "fully utilizing two markets and two resources".

The second aspect is the mixed strategy of export-oriented (EOI) and import-substitution industrialization (ISI). China's policy formulation seems not to get tangled in the ongoing debate between EOI and ISI strategies. In the light of the pragmatic principle, China does not go for the whole set of recommendations of either ISI or EOI but chose to develop a mixed strategy. On the one hand, it fully utilized its abundant factors like labour and land and well-designed policy like processing trade to develop a quite strong export sector, for example, textile in the 1980s, to accumulate finance through trade revenue. On the other hand, through policy push like R&D coordination or technology transfer, China avoided being static locked-in. Further, China rapidly developed its high-tech industry and diversified its economy, making itself a leading exporter in broad manufacturing products with high ECI.

3.4 Conclusion and Way Forward

In an ancient Chinese book, ***Spring and Autumn Annals of Master Yan*** (***Yanzi Chunqiu***), Yan Ying, prime minister of the Qi State in Zhou Dynasty, used the following metaphor: "Tangerines in Huainan (the south of Huai river) are big and sweet, but once tangerine trees are planted in Huaibei (the north of Huai river), they can only bear small and bitter fruits, though the leaves look similar. Why? Because the environment differs". This metaphor may also explain the distinct effectiveness of similar economic policies in different countries or different times.

In this chapter, we have focused on China's industrial policies, which has undoubtedly played a vital role in driving China's structural transformation and industrialization since 1978. China's policy lessons and experiences could significantly contribute to development thinking, particularly regarding the state's role in economic growth. They may also provide some pragmatic reference points for the policy formulation of other developing countries. However, as Yan Ying's metaphor indicates, policymakers should not pursue automatically "the best" experiences or panacea for economic growth but keep exploring, testing, and adjusting the policies and practices to discover approaches that are most suitable to their local circumstances. That perhaps is the essence of all successful stories of economic development.

CHAPTER 4
Global Value Chains and Development - Lessons from China's Integration Strategy

Chapter 4: Global Value Chains and Development - Lessons from China's Integration Strategy

4.1 Introduction[32]

The world economy is at a critical crossroad. The COVID-19 shock and the self-induced economic crisis that followed caused an unprecedented global recession, the most severe after the second world war. Particularly felt by developing economies and LDCs, these impacts are combined with long-lasting challenges and the fallouts of the 2008 global financial crisis. In such a challenging and uncertain environment, the development strategies followed by successful catch-up countries until the recent past have become by far less effective. The role of trade in spurring industrialization and development is no longer what it used to be during the East Asian miracle when it aided economic take-off and the achievement of unprecedented and sustained growth.

Today's global economy is, in fact, a much more open and contested space than the 1960s, when the East Asian late industrializers began their successful "catch-up" growth experience. Differences stem not only from their successful trajectories but also from the subsequent liberalization drive across the world through multilateral, regional, and bilateral trade and investment agreements. Another distinction arises from the entry of former centrally planned economies into the global trading system with a concomitant rise in the global supply of unskilled and semi-skilled labour. With a multitude of countries simultaneously trying to realize the promise of export-led industrialization, competition has intensified in activities that rely on unskilled labour.

At another level, the resulting international division of labour has become a more managed space. New information and communication technologies (ICTs), stronger intellectual property rights, combined with weakened labour laws have shifted the balance of economic power towards larger firms with dominant market positions and an attendant ability to generate super-profits (UNCTAD, 2017). In the face of fewer restrictions on how these firms can move capital across borders, not only has it become easier and cheaper to organise far-flung production networks but to govern those networks in ways that further skew the benefits in favour of leading firms. Therefore, integration into these networks alone cannot guarantee the capturing of significant development dividends, and success is rather related to the *type* of integration achieved. Countries able to develop productive capacities in synchronization with those needed by global value chains (GVCs) and position themselves at a relatively high level in the world's distribution of tasks should be well placed to sustain a more inclusive growth process. To do so, adopting a set of trade and industrial measures tailored to local conditions and capabilities,

---

[32] This chapter is prepared by Piergiuseppe Fortunato based on a background paper written by Zhang Jianping (2021), "Strengthen the structural transformation of the Belt and Road partner countries: global value chain integration and upgrade" https://unctad.org/system/files/official-document/BRI-Project_RP12_en.pdf

and staying tuned to biases and asymmetries in the external environment are practices of primary importance.

China represents a remarkable example in this respect. The country launched an ambitious process of gradual reforms and progressive opening-up of the economy in 1978 and sustained impressive growth performance for over four decades. China has now become the second-largest economy in the world after the United States. And while in 1949 the Chinese GDP was less than 2 per cent of the American's, by 2018, this ratio increased to 64 per cent. Despite the specificities of the Chinese economy and the obvious difficulties that any country would encounter when applying specific devised measures, important lessons emerge from the Chinese experience on the philosophical approach to industrial policymaking in a fast-changing global scenario and on the general pillars for a successful integration and development strategy.

This chapter presents some of the main challenges and opportunities faced by developing economies at the time of globalization of production in section 4.2; section 4.3 discusses the Chinese successful policy experience, and section 4.4 aims at pinning down few core lessons that could be used as a reference point for policymakers of the South.

4.2 GVCs, Industrialization and Development

Figure 4.1: Share of merchandise exports in world GDP, 1970–2016

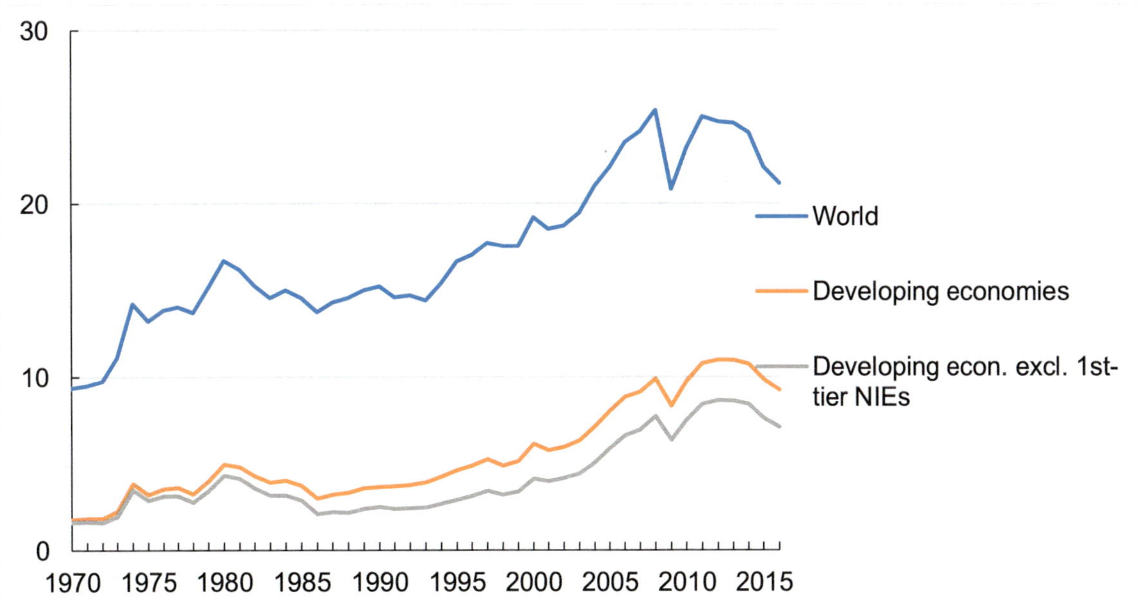

Source: Braunstein et al. (2019).

The global economy and the organization of international production and trade have changed significantly in the last three decades. These changes have a quantitative dimension reflected in the steadily rising share of trade in the world output. Initially, this tendency manifested amongst advanced economies, but since the early 1970s and more sharply the early 1990s, the developing countries share of world trade has also risen steadily (Figure 4.1). But the qualitative change in that organization is seen by many as even more significant, with the structuring of the global economy around GVCs, whereby multi-national enterprises (MNEs) break up the production process into constituent parts and locate them across multiple national and continental boundaries. As a result, goods (and some services) are no longer simply made in one country and shipped to another for sale. Instead, goods go through many stages, each associated with a specific task, traversing several geographic and organizational borders and adding components and value before reaching their final markets.

Figure 4.2 depicts changes in Foreign Value Added (FVA) between 1995 and 2011. FVA is the value-added generated outside the country where the last production stage takes place before the product is sold (the so-called country-of-completion). The figure shows that, over the last decades, the foreign content of exports has increased significantly in many regions, particularly in Asia but also in Europe and North America. Foreign content shares, for example, doubled over the period in India, Poland, Turkey, Korea, and Vietnam. It has trebled in Cambodia, with significant increases also observed in OECD economies, such as Germany, whose foreign content share increased by 10 percentage points, up to 25% in 2011. It is worth noting that, on this measure, the variation in both levels of participation and the changes over time are considerable.

Figure 4.2: Foreign value-added as percentage of gross export, selected economies, 1995–2011

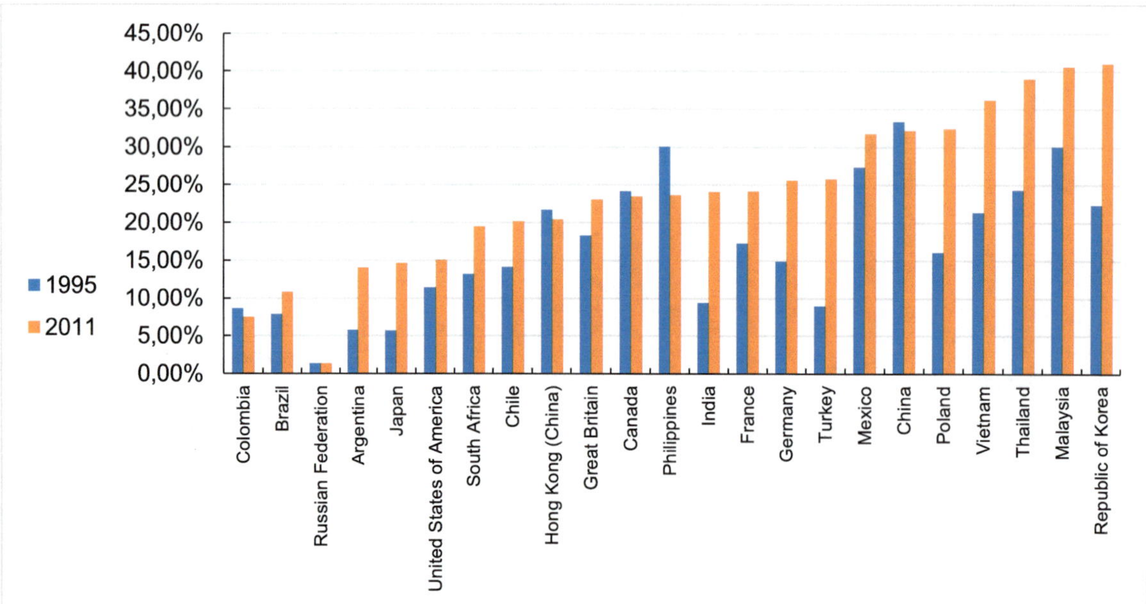

Source: Braunstein et al. (2019).

The emergence and expansion of GVCs are often presented as the natural outcome of an open global trading system and a promising basis for further trade and investment liberalization (OECD, 2013; WTO et al., 2013). Efforts to manage or roll them back are seen as naïve at best and more likely damaging to economic and social progress (Lamy, 2006). From a development perspective, participation in GVCs is seen as an attainable first step towards export-oriented industrialization. Rather than developing an entire product or breaking into an extremely competitive market on their own, countries can specialize in specific tasks or components of a multitude of value chains, starting at the relatively accessible bottom.

The limits of this approach have long been understood in the context of commodity-exporting, given the weak linkage and spillover effects associated with commodity chains. The evidence for a positive causal connection between GVC participation and industrialization is not much better (Kozul-Wright and Fortunato, 2019; UNCTAD, 2014). Going beyond the primary sector, UNCTAD (2016) shows that only when increases in the foreign value-added of exports occur in a larger context of greater production and exports of manufactures can GVC participation complement industrialization and structural change. Conversely, when increasing participation in GVCs reflects a reduction of domestic sourcing in a context of weak export performance of manufactures, GVC participation may even delay structural transformation.

This is illustrated in Figure 4.3, which plots the association between changes in manufacturing value-added as a share of GDP and changes in the import content of export-oriented manufactures (i.e., foreign value addition) between 1995 and 2011, for Asian economies and the remaining developing countries and economies in transition when data are available.

Figure 4.3: Changes in the shares of foreign value-added in manufacturing exports and manufacturing value-added in GDP, selected economies, 1995–2011

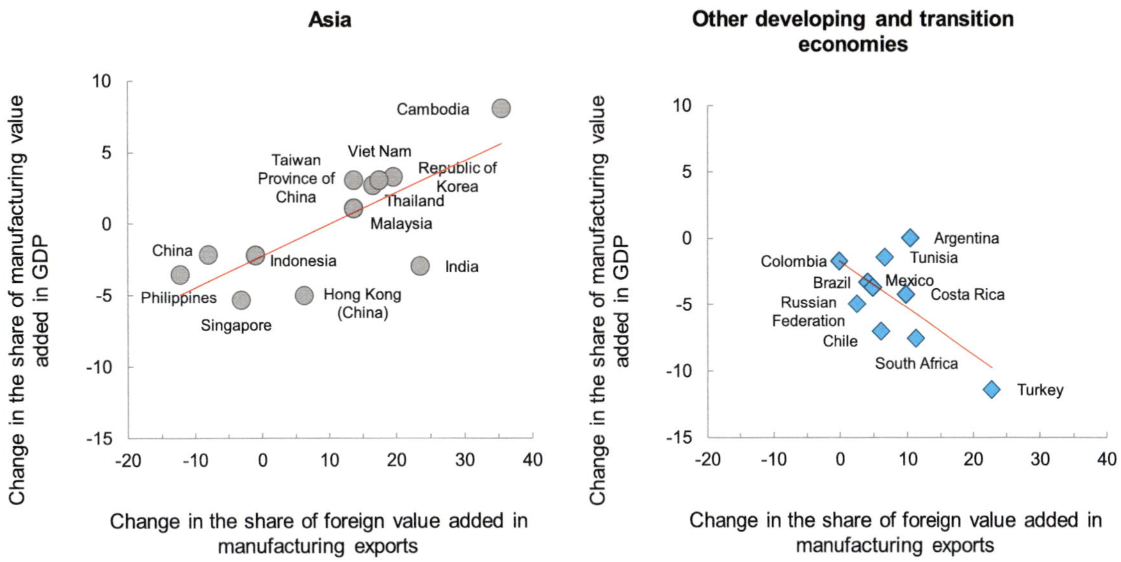

Source: UNCTAD (2016).

Many countries in Asia show a clear, strong, and positive association between GVC participation and industrialization. On the other hand, developing countries in other regions show the opposite relationship, as evidenced by the negative slope of the fitted value-line for other developing countries in Figure 4.3.

Claims that GVCs strengthen productivity or contribute to growth are still largely based on conventional trade models (see, for instance, OECD, 2013). But from the trade and development linkages point of view, the particularities of GVC structures and the consequent distribution of power along the value chain require a more specific analysis. On the one hand, GVCs lower barriers to entry at the bottom of the value chain, making it easier for developing countries to break into global manufacturing exports than in the past. However, the conditions that ease access can also act as barriers to upgrading. More accessible parts of the value chain are associated with few forward and backward linkages, limited institutional development, and remote possibility for knowledge externalities in the wider economy. Therefore, developing economies with limited productive capacities can remain trapped in, and competing for, the lowest value-adding activities, resulting in "thin industrialization" and slow economic growth (Gereffi, 2014; UNCTAD 2015). These activities are also detrimental from a dynamic perspective since they do not generate those local productive capacities, which are essential to meaningful development.

Additionally, Participation in GVCs also carries the risk of specialization in only a very narrow strand of production with a concomitantly narrow technological base and overdependence on MNEs for market access. Hyper-specialization appears to have accompanied the pick-up of trade flows in developing countries from the 1990s (Hanson, 2005; OECD et al., 2013). This circumstance, in part, reflects the reversion in many countries to primary export dependence against the backdrop of rising commodity prices from the start of the millennium. But it is also a reflection of asymmetric power relations between leading firms and suppliers in manufacturing activities and the overall weak bargaining positions of developing countries, particularly in countries experiencing premature deindustrialization.

The experiences of Mexico and Central American countries as assembly manufacturers, for example, have been linked to the creation of an enclave economy, with few domestic linkages (Gallagher and Zarsky, 2007; Paus, 2014). The same can be said about the electronics and automotive industries in Eastern and Central Europe (Plank and Staritz, 2013; Pavlinek, 2015; Pavlinek and Zenka, 2016). Although this situation has not ruled out "internal upgrading" within MNE affiliates, it has generated very few spillovers to the domestic economy in productivity improvements and imitation by domestic firms, partly due to limited linkages of MNEs with local firms and labour markets (Fons-Rosen et al., 2013; Paus, 2014).

4.3 Turning GVCs into an Engine of Development: Lessons from China

As demonstrated in the previous section, targeting the growth of export-oriented manufactures or increasing participation in GVCs offers neither automatic nor straightforward pathways to industrialization and development. This finding, however, does not imply that countries should no longer seek export markets and productive integration. Instead, a more strategic approach is needed in which countries are more selective in their choices of processes, products, and markets. Such an approach is especially relevant since both the composition of export-oriented manufactures – the more technologically intensive and sophisticated, the better – and the share of domestic value-added determine whether and to what extent exporting will induce structural change and productivity growth (Hausmann et al. 2007, and Fortunato and Razo, 2014).

The type of participation in GVCs is crucial in this respect. In fact, only those countries able to position themselves at a relatively high level in the world distribution of tasks are likely to obtain significant development dividends from GVCs participation. However, simply complying with the demands of leading firms in these chains is unlikely to facilitate the emergence of the kind of industrial base necessary for sustained growth and inclusive development. There is little evidence of technological and other spillovers from MNEs in the absence of effective government policy measures, even when greenfield investments have involved a fuller range of industrial activities, and evidence of upgrading within value chains is equally elusive. Therefore, a 'developmental state' has a critical role to play, especially favouring the emergence of a vibrant industrial base, a dynamic corporate sector, and continuous upgrading along value chains (Kozul-Wright and Fortunato, 2015; UNCTAD, 2016).

China undoubtedly represents a successful example in this respect. Over the last three decades, the country managed to harness increasing participation in GVCs. At first, it became a processing and assembly hub and later transformed itself into an innovation centre and a global supplier of research and development, technology intensive parts, and components (Figure 4). Its experience offers important lessons for other developing economies struggling to climb up the ladders in the international division of labour and transform their productive structures.

Figure 4.4: China's processing trade development development

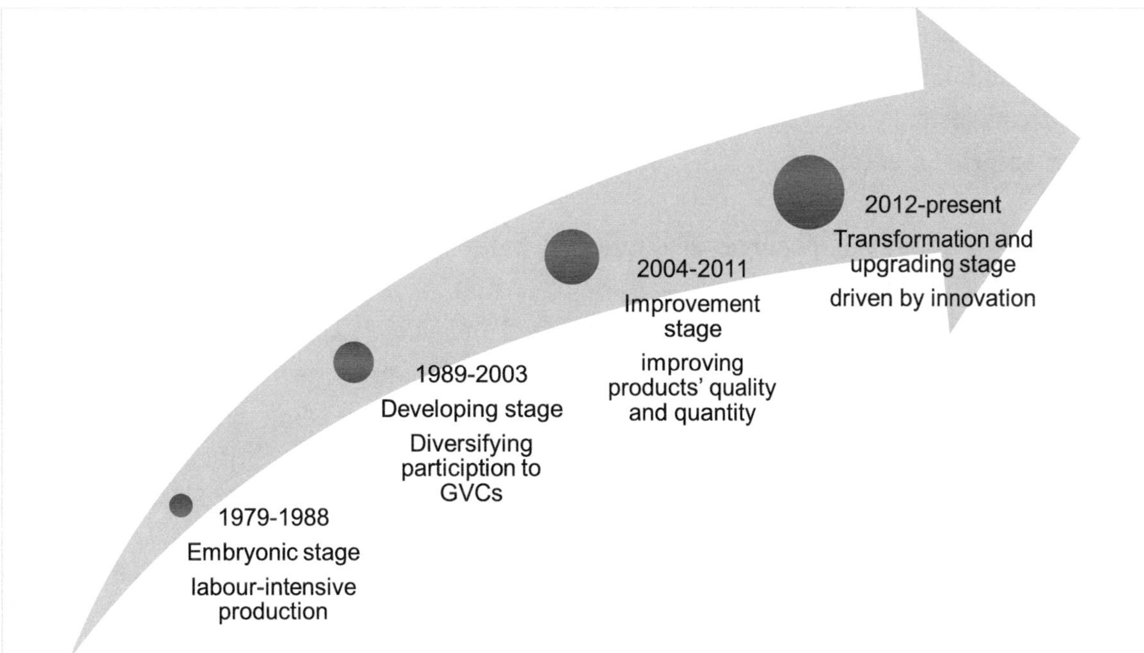

Source: author's graphical elaboration.

This chapter is devoted to discussing some of the critical pillars of the Chinese development and integration strategy in the remaining parts. Further, this chapter identifies vital lessons learnt over the years.

4.3.1 Gradualism and Experimentation

Along with the reform process, China invariably took strategic decisions suitable to its level of development and based on the principles of gradualism and experimentation. Since the beginning of the reform in 1978, the country has gone through four different and progressively more ambitious phases: (i) Market-for-capital and Accumulating Trade Surplus (1979-1992); (ii) Radical Export-Oriented Strategy (1993-2001); (iii) Liberalized Export-Oriented Strategy (2002-2012); and (iv) Equal import and export, the two-way investment strategy (2013-present).

China embarked on the first phase of the reforms with a low level of social productivity and a marginal position in the global trading system. By 1992, the overall development level and the productive capacity had substantially improved. At this stage, the foreign trade strategy evolved into a radical export-oriented strategy. Finally, the comprehensive opening strategy was based on the decrease in global demand after the financial crisis, which made exporting more difficult and increased domestic demand. This strategy paid equal attention to import and export and two-way investment that started to be implemented all around China in 2012.

The use of pilot provinces to test new policy measures before comprehensive implementation (at different speeds across regions at different socio-economic levels of development) is another peculiar feature of the Chinese policy approach. In the last twenty years, four special economic zones (including Shenzhen) were gradually expanded to 14 coastal cities and more peripheral regions. In the 21st century, China has continued promoting the development of industrial parks and bonded zone strategy even more vigorously. New Free Trade Zones (FTZs) have been established from Shanghai, Tianjin, Guangdong and Fujian, to Hainan island, Shandong, and Hebei provinces.

The strategy of the gradual opening is also reflected in the specific policy measures adopted to support export activities. In the forty years of reform and opening up, China moved from preferential policies such as taxation and granting land and finance access to attracting foreign investment with a fair, competitive and open business environment; from gradually reducing tariffs after joining the WTO to facilitating investment and trade, speeding up the reform of the public administration and delegate powers. Overall, the opening strategy shifted its focus from GVCs participation to upgrading and finally constructing China's headquartered regional and global production networks.

4.3.2 A Combination of Bringing in and Going Global

Bringing in (mainly FDI) and Going Global are important aspects of China's economic growth and integration into global value chains. Inward FDI promoted the transformation of domestic industries and offered opportunities to modernize the industrial system and improve manufacturing enterprises' production technology and managerial capabilities. Going global, and investing abroad, in turn, enabled Chinese companies to participate directly in the operation of global value chains by actively seeking natural resources, market opportunities and strategic resources.

By gradually adjusting the so-called *Catalogue of Industries to Encourage Investment*, the list of strategically targeted sectors, China shifted its target from attracting investment in the light textile manufacturing industry to FDI in manufacturing, and finally in high-tech. While improving the quality of inward FDI, China has also accelerated the pace of outward FDI that sustained China's integration into global production. With the continuous improvement of China's industrial system and corporate competitiveness, China began implementing its Going Global strategy in 2003. The government mainly promoted the construction of overseas economic and trade cooperation zones, cross-border economic cooperation zones, border economic cooperation zones, and other platforms. More recently, the government launched the Belt and Road Initiative (BRI) to facilitate connections with other developing economies and advance new RVCs.

Figure 4.5: Inward and outward FDI, China, 1983–2016, USD billion

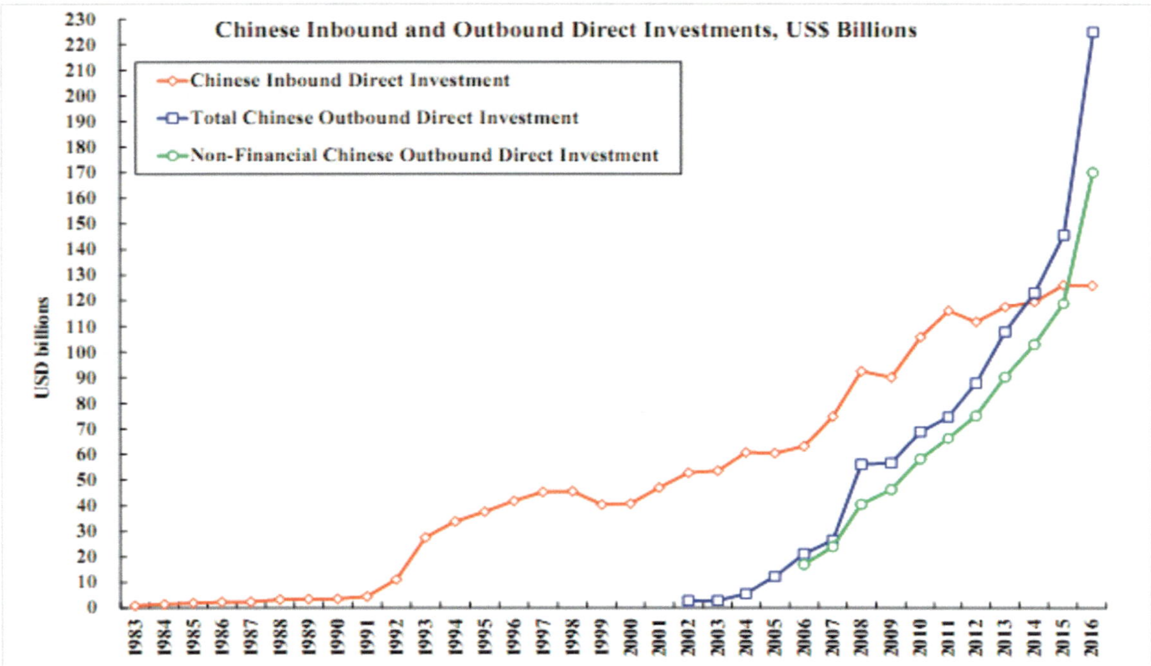

Source: Statistical bulletins on China's outbound direct investment over the years.

4.3.3 Taking Full Advantage of the Demographic Dividend

Along the impressive development pattern followed in the last decades, China also seized its demographic transition, managing to improve its positioning in the international division of labour. Initially, China exploited its abundance of labour, and its relatively low costs, to forge a comparative advantage in production, processing, and assembly activities, which facilitated its integration into international production networks. In fact, since the 1970s, as China's demographic transition entered the low fertility/low mortality stage, the population dependency ratio declined rapidly, and the size of the labour force increased (Figure 4.6). During the same period, China introduced the household contract responsibility system and gradually released excess labour from agriculture. The reform of state-owned enterprises had a similar impact channelling human capital and labour towards the most productive firms in the private sector.

The benefits of the Demographic Dividend were felt, especially after joining the WTO in 2001. Over the last decade, the Chinese business environment further improved, and the efficiency of labour resources increased, under the promotion of supply-side structural reform, high-quality development and other strategies. As a consequence, the positioning of China in the global value chain constantly improved.

Figure 4.6: Demographic dividend, China, 1976–2018

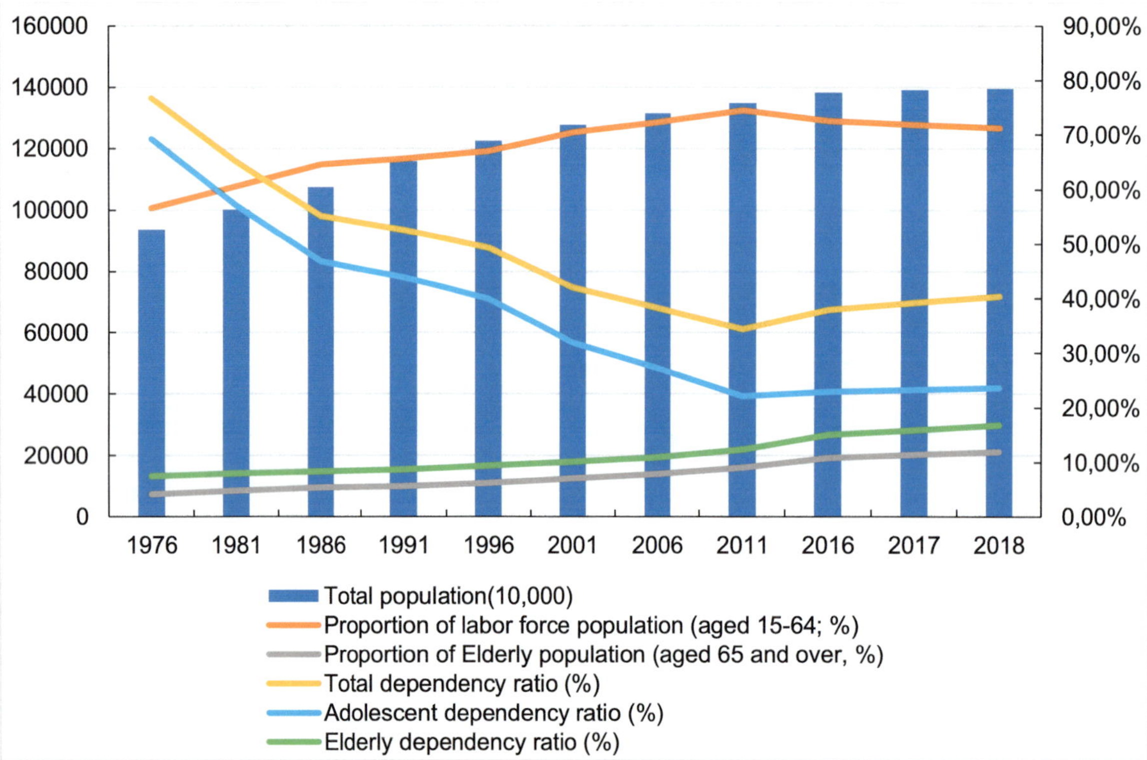

Source: Database of the statistics bureau of the People's Republic of China.

4.3.4 Investing in Infrastructures

China integration into global value chains and rapid economic growth is inseparable from large-scale infrastructure projects such as transportation, energy, and power grid. Infrastructure is critical to improve the business environment, promote inter-regional coordination, and alleviate the mismatch of factors, thereby sustaining long-term economic growth. Transportation infrastructures favour the migration of labour, and more generally, the movement of production factors and reduce the transportation costs faced by enterprises. Information infrastructure, in turn, facilitates industrial integration, boosts labour productivity, and aids the manufacturing industry to move up the value chain.

Since the early stages of the reform, China carried out large-scale transportation infrastructure projects and gradually built a network of railways, highways, aviation, and maritime infrastructure to reach the whole country and effectively connect the country with the rest of the world (Figure 4.7). This infrastructure significantly improved the interconnection and communication of people and promoted the flow of goods.

China also made remarkable achievements in power supply and power grid construction. By the end of 2017, the total installed power generation capacity nationwide was 1,77,703,000 kilowatts, more than 30 times that of 1978. The total length of power transmission lines above 220 kilovolts reached 688,000 kilometres, 30 times that of 1978. At the same time, the scale of China's power grid ranked uninterruptedly first in the world since 2005.

Figure 4.7: Transportation infrastructure development, China, 1978–2018

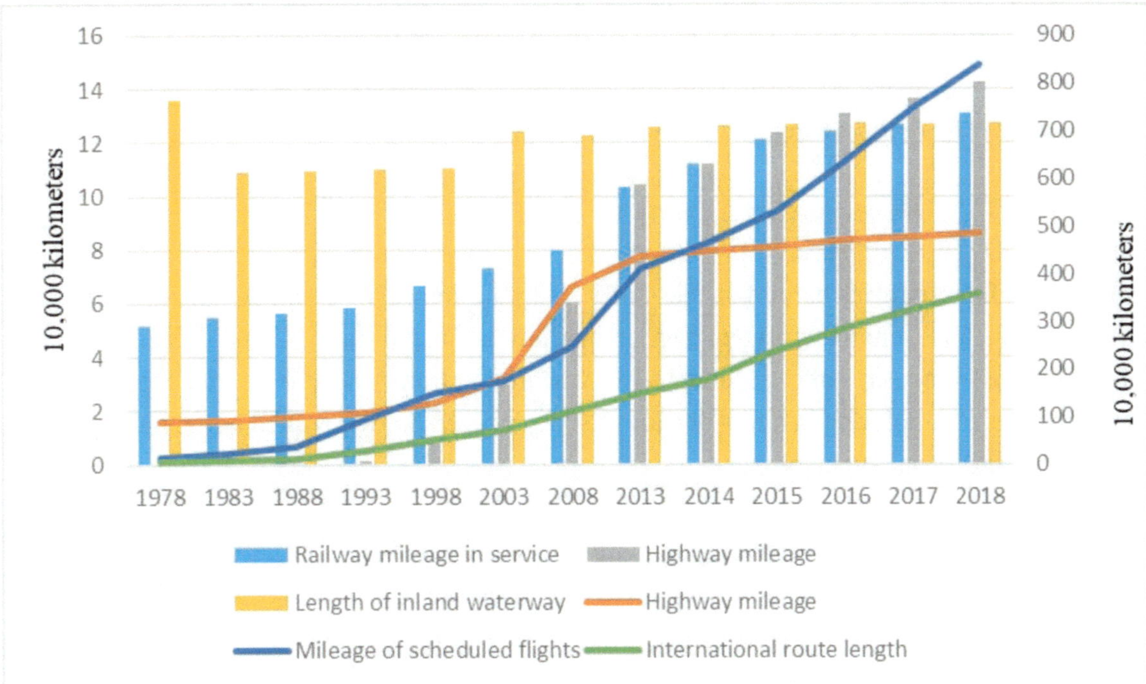

Source: Database of the statistics bureau of the People's Republic of China.

Finally, since the late 1980s, and even more in the first two decades of the 21st century, China has made great progress in information and communication infrastructure. At the end of March 2019, the total length of the national optical cable line reached 44.71 million kilometres, while 15 years earlier, in 2005, it was only 4.07 million kilometres. The total number of mobile communication base stations reached 6.62 million, and the number of internet access terminals reached 889 million. The rapid development of China's communication network infrastructure promoted the rapid rise of telephone and internet penetration as well as the number of internet users (see Figure 4.8). This underlying communication infrastructure represents an important basis for fostering continuous production upgrading and promoting the development of the internet economy, big data, the internet of things, and artificial intelligence in the new digital era.

Figure 4.8: Telecommunications and Internet infrastructure development, China, 1999–2018

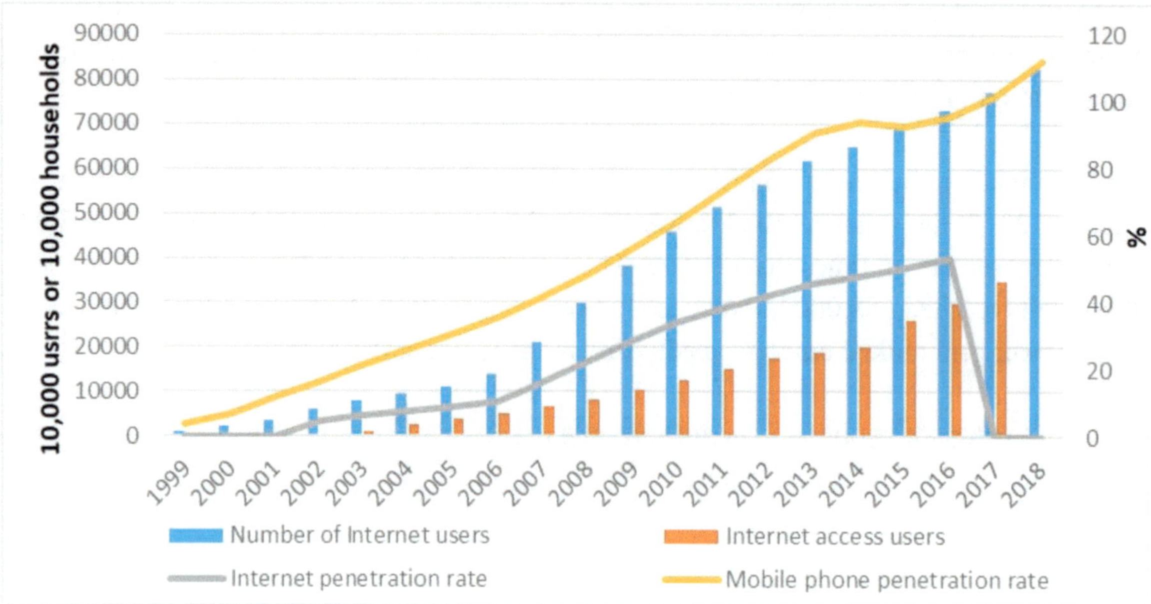

Source: Database of the statistics bureau of the People's Republic of China.

4.3.5 Climbing the value chain ladder

Large developing countries cannot successfully integrate into GVCs and advance towards the higher-end of those chains without fast industrialization. In fact, China experienced an unprecedented process of accelerated structural transformation and progressive industrialization, completing in a few decades a successful transition from a largely agricultural country to an industrial super-power.

In 1978, China was still a predominantly agricultural country, with the primary sector accounting for 47.7% of the GDP. The population employed in agriculture was 70.5%, while total imports and exports accounted only for 9.7% of GDP. At the same time, the industrial system was still in the initial stage of industrialization. Forty years later, in 2018, the GDP of the secondary industry reached 36.6 trillion RMB, 209 times that of 1978. China has developed into one of the few countries with a complete and fully diversified industrial structure, with 39 macro industrial categories, 191 micro categories, 525 sub-categories. In addition, the country provides more than 80% of the world's medium and low-end manufacturing products (Table 4.1).

Along with the industrialization process, government guidance was of critical importance. The government shaped the industrial structure by adopting selective industrial policies. In particular, support was provided to strategic infant industries through taxation policies and privileged access to land and capital. In the early stage of the reform process, the *Six Priority Policies* package was implemented to support the textile industry. The package focused on capital, foreign exchange, technology, infrastructure and transportation, and promoted labour-intensive industries. The policy approach changed in the last two decades: China's main tool of intervention became the formulation of industry guidance catalogues, such as Catalogue of

Industries, Products and Technologies Currently Encouraged by the State (2000), the Catalogue of Eliminating Outdated Production Capacity, Processes and Products (2002), the Industrial Structure Adjustment Guidance Catalogue (2005, 2009, 2011), among others. These catalogues essentially promoted the effective allocation of resources to the identified priority industries.

Table 4.1: Comparison of economic structure between 1978 and 2018, China

Index	*1978*	*1978*	*2018*	*2018*	*Index*
	Number of employed people (10,000 people)	*Gross domestic product, 100 million yuan (percentage)*	*Number of employed people (10,000 people)*	*Gross domestic product, 100 million yuan (% of weight)*	*Employment (2018/ 1978)*
National	40152	3678.7	77586	900309	1.93
Primary industry	28318	1018.5 (27.7%)	20257.7	64734 (7.2%)	0.72
Secondary industry	6945	1755.2 (47.7%)	21390.5	366000.9 (40.7%)	3.08
Tertiary Industry	4980	905.1 (24.6%)	35937.8	469574.6 (52.2%)	7.22
Per capita GDP		385.0 (yuan)	64644 (yuan)		

Source: Database of the statistics bureau of the People's Republic of China.

China also continuously adjusted its industrial policy stance and balanced industrial and competition policies, aiming at upgrading its industrial base. With the continuous improvement of the industrial system, the government gradually reduced its intervention. It shifted to policies that promote competition and encourage innovation, such as technological innovation, supporting the transformation of scientific and technological achievements, encouraging the marketization of production factors, protecting patents and intellectual property rights, etc. The implementation of these policies effectively promoted technological progress, improved industrial efficiency and enabled the upgrading of industrial structure.

Finally, as mentioned above, during industrialization, the creation of industrial parks has played a critical role. These parks actually succeeded because their characteristics were different across countries and regions, such as the Pearl River Delta Model, Southern Jiangsu Model, Wenzhou Model, etc. All the parks promoted local industrialization, but considering regional conditions, specific firms were supported and some particular policy instruments were adapted.

4.3.6 Building a National Innovation System

Over the last four decades, China has significantly improved its production technology and innovation capability by introducing advanced foreign technology and constantly increasing its investment in science, technology, and human capital formation. This approach allowed the country to gradually narrow down the technological divide vis-a-vis more advanced economies.

In the first stages of the reform process, the Government directly guided scientific and technological innovation through strategic planning. In a second phase, from 1998 to 2006, with the acceleration of globalization, China aimed at rejuvenating and upgrading the growing workforce through massive investment in science and education. More recently, since 2006, a policy set-up focusing on "independent innovation, key leapfrogging, supporting development, and leading the future" was enacted. Finally, in 2012 China embraced a full-fledged innovation-driven development strategy, culminated in 2016 with the adoption of the strategic goal of becoming the world leader in science and innovation by 2050.

The development of a national innovation system leaned since the incept on embedding science and technology within the economic and productive structure of the country, strengthening the active role of innovation subjects, and investing in the training of scientific and technological personnel. Technological innovation was also sustained through strategic foreign investment attraction policies, which favoured a gradual evolution from the adaptation of traditional technology to independent research and development of core technologies.

In terms of instruments, during the first phases (1978-1986), income tax reductions and different forms of conditionalities were used to encourage the introduction of world advanced technologies, mainly through joint ventures. From 1987 to 1993, special economic zones and high-tech development zones were used as platforms to introduce advanced foreign technologies. High-tech enterprises operating in these zones were granted preferential treatment in terms of taxation, import and export facilitation, and pricing policies, which greatly improved the speed of technology introduction.

During the so-called improvement phase (1994-2001), policies were formulated based on the differences in production technologies and quality standards in different industries to encourage foreign companies to carry out technological transformation and upgrading in China. After China's accession to the WTO (2001-2012), the policy stance encouraged the establishment of R&D institutions overseas and R&D alliances. Finally, in the last years (2013-now), the government aims to strengthen the cooperation between different R&D institutions (cross-fertilization) and facilitate independent research and development and intellectual property protection.

Another pillar of the Chinese innovation model is the promotion of Enterprise-University-Research Institute cooperation with various policy tools. China adopted supply-oriented policies (based on technology capital investment, scientific and technological personnel development and technology infrastructure construction), environmental policies (regulations, tax incentives, financial support and intellectual property protection) and demand-oriented policies (government procurement and transformation of scientific and technological achievements).

In the early stages of the development of Enterprise-university-research institute cooperation, China encouraged tripartite cooperation through regulation and direct expansion of supply. Before 2006, policy tools mainly included investment in science and technology, cultivation of scientific and technological talents, and tax incentives. During the take-off, environment-oriented and demand-oriented policies were mainly applied, which was reflected in the use of a large number of regulatory policy tools since 2006. Meanwhile, financial support and intellectual property protection were incrementally reinforced. From 2006 to 2008, government procurement, service outsourcing, trade controls, and policy tools for overseas institutions were increased. After 2008, policy tools supporting the transformation of scientific and technological achievements continued to grow (Figure 4.9).

Figure 4.9: Enterprises-University-research institutes cooperation policy tools, China, 1999–2005/2006–2014

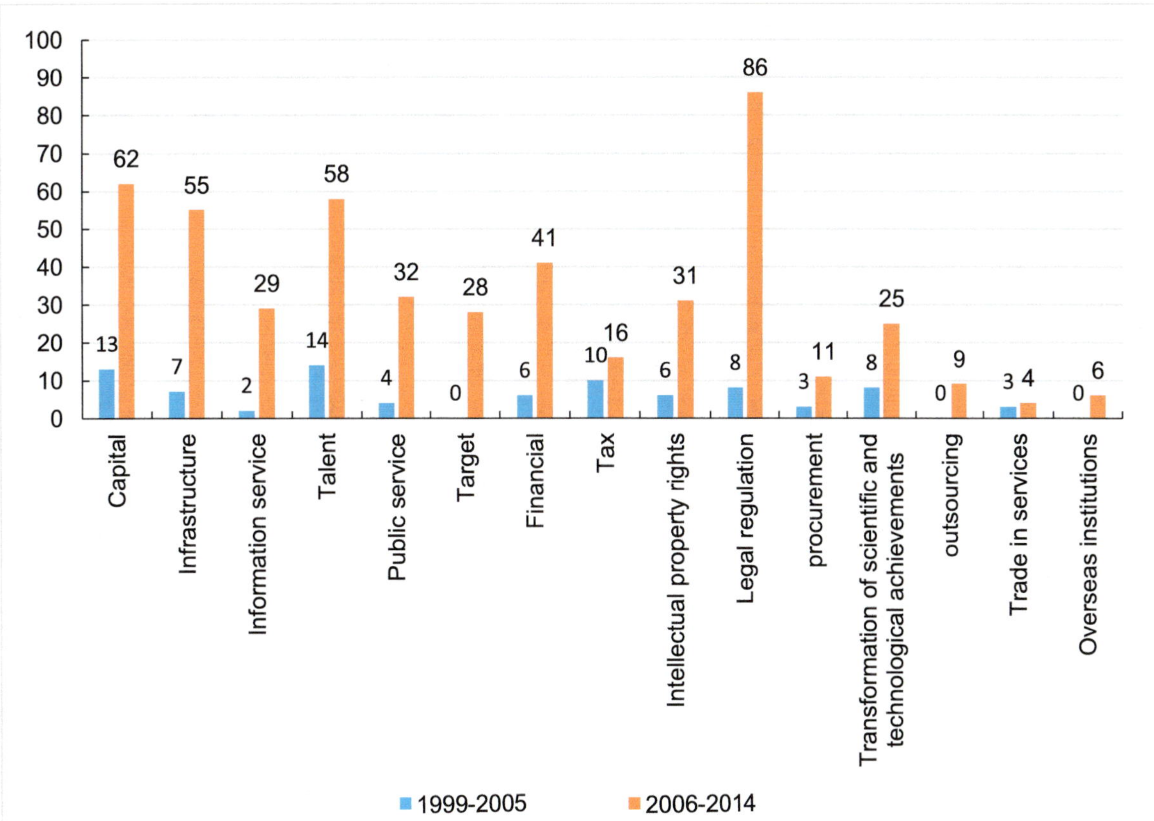

4.4 Policy Conclusions

Today, policymakers can no longer expect that the export-led production and manufacturing trade that fueled industrialization in the East Asian Tigers will produce similar outcomes.

Indeed, increasing participation in GVCs offers neither an automatic nor a straightforward pathway to industrialization. A more conscious and strategic approach to productive integration is required, where the quality of integration matters as much as its quantity.

As the Chinese experience discussed in the previous section testifies, a comprehensive policy strategy needs to be gradual and to evolve over time, showing the ability to adapt both to technological changes and to local conditions and circumstances (Andreoni and Chang, 2016, and Staritz, et al., 2016). Nevertheless, China has continuously employed traditional instruments – such as subsidies and regulations - to support domestic productive capacity and state-owned financial institutions to mobilize and allocate savings, secure profitability, socialize risks, and facilitate the internalization of new technologies.

It also needs to use public-sector procurement policies to support strategic sectors and public investment to promote R&D and remove bottlenecks, especially in infrastructure and basic industries. Such a policy framework also requires competition rules and targeted policies to restrict market power, manage entry into key growth sectors, address coordination failures and regulate the ownership of productive assets, including intellectual property, to support investment and innovation and maximize learning spillovers. Finally, targeted measures to generate an appropriately qualified labour force through training and education programmes are crucial. The selection of relevant sectors and industries for support should obviously vary from country to country (and along the process of development) according to the areas of strengths and potential for upgrading, dynamic comparative advantage and, in the larger economies, the creation of national champions that can become major players in the international markets.

Unfortunately, with respect to the initial phases of Chinese take-off, trade and investment agreements at the bilateral, regional, and multilateral levels have subsequently restricted policy space in some key areas (Wade, 2003, and UNCTAD, 2014). The COVID-19 shock, and the global depression that it triggered, are constraining even more export possibilities. In such a difficult external environment, South-South cooperation opens up new opportunities to overcome the existing constraints and bolster regional trade and productive integration, instrumental to structural transformation.

China's Belt and Road Initiative (BRI) exemplifies the role that closer integration and cooperation among developing countries can play to overcome the obstacles hindering development in vast parts of the Global South. The initiative can facilitate the deployment of financing mechanisms for trade and infrastructure development, promote the formation of new supply chain and production networks, and offer better opportunities for developing countries to fruitfully integrate into the international division of labour.

CHAPTER 5
China's Digital Transformation: Learnings for the Developing countries

Chapter 5: China's Digital Transformation: Learnings for the Developing countries

5.1 Introduction[33]

The pandemic outbreak has highlighted the importance of building the digital economy, especially in the global south. Many developing countries and most of the LDCs lag even in terms of basic ICT infrastructure, which is internet access to their population. This situation has led Covid-19 to economically hurt the Global South more than the developed world. In order to revive their adversely impacted industry and trade, developing countries need to revisit their trade and industrial policies with a greater focus on the digital economy.

There is a need for developing countries to design a comprehensive national policy for building their digital economy with targeted strategies at the sub-national level. Both demand and supply-side constraints need to be addressed. China provides a successful example of a developing country that has been able to digitally transform itself from a manufacturing assembly hub to a digital power. While it may not be possible for developing countries to replicate China's policy experience, many policy lessons can help developing countries design policies to be successfully implemented and support the progress towards sustainable development goals.

The digital economy has played a key role in building China's export competitiveness and in its industrialization efforts. Within a couple of decades, China has emerged from a global assembly hub to a digital giant and has become a lead firm developing its own global and regional value chains. In 2016, China's digital economy valued US$3.4 trillion, accounting for 30% of the total GDP, comparing favourably to many of the developing countries like Brazil, India, Indonesia, with digital economy contributing 21 per cent, 18 per cent and 11 per cent respectively. However, the digital economy's contribution averaged around 50 per cent in developed countries like the US, Germany, and the UK. Although the size of China's digital economy was only 32 per cent of the size of the US's digital economy, it was growing at an average annual rate close to 19 per cent, more than three times that of the US, which was around 6 per cent. The digital economy's contribution to China's GDP growth in 2016 was around 60 per cent, and henceforth it has become the new driver of its economic growth.

This chapter highlights China's successful digital transformation by examining trends in some of the key indicators digital economy's growth. Drawing from He and Sun (2020), it shares

[33] This chapter is prepared by Rashmi Banga and is based on the papers undertaken by He Wei and Sun Xin (2020), "China's Policy Practice for Digital Economy Development" and Chen (2020) "The Development of China's Digital Economy: A Study on China's E-Commerce Development and Policy Implications" available at https://unctad.org/en/PublicationsLibrary/BRI-Project_RP2_en.pdf and https://unctad.org/en/PublicationsLibrary/BRI-Project_RP3_en.pdf

some of the key policies that helped build China's digital economy, particularly in building network infrastructure, accelerating deep integration of the internet with the real economy, and enhancing information technology capabilities. Data has been recognized as a critical resource by China, and accordingly, data governance policies have also played a strategic role in building China's digital economy. The chapter also shares China's successful experience of building its e-commerce sector. As a case study, it traces the growth of one of the most successful China's e-commerce platforms, which is Alibaba. Drawing from the paper undertaken by Chen (2020), the chapter traces the growth of Alibaba and identifies some of the government's core policies that helped create a digital ecosystem and facilitated Alibaba's growth. These include putting in place inclusive and prudent regulations, developing a robust digital infrastructure and encouraging entrepreneurship and innovations.

The remaining parts of the chapter are organized as follows: section 5.2 provides trends in key indicators of China's digital economy growth; section 5.3 outlines some of the crucial digital policies implemented by China and section 5.4 presents indicators for its successful implementation; section 5.5 shares the policies put in place to help the growth of e-commerce platforms, with particular emphasis on the growth experience of Alibaba; section 5.6 provides details of China's data governance policies and regulations; section 5.7 concludes by drawing key lessons from China's policy experiences for other developing countries and provides a way forward for them.

5.2 Key Indicators of Growth in Digital Economy

Over time, China's successful digital transformation is evident from the trends on different growth indicators of its digital economy (Table 5.1). China compares favourably with other developing countries, especially the BRICS, on almost all indicators of digital economy growth. It ranks higher than India and South Africa regarding the ICT Development Index and has a larger number of fixed broadband subscriptions (per 100 inhabitants) than other BRICS countries.

According to the OECD Economic Surveys of China, the size of China's digital economy in 2016 was USD 3.4 trillion, which was 30.3% of its GDP (Table 5.2). The size of China's digital economy is only second to the US's digital economy and bigger than the rest of the countries in the world. In terms of the digital economy's share in GDP, it is around 50% for major developed countries such as the U.S., Germany, and the U.K. and approximately 17.8% for India, 20.9% for Brazil, and 11% for Indonesia.

Table 5.1: Existing digital capacity, BRICS and Advanced Countries, 2017

	Number of internet users in selected countries as of 2017 (in millions)	*ICT Development Index Ranking (IDI)*	*Fixed Broadband Subscriptions per 100 inhabitants*	*Active Mobile-broadband subscription per 100 inhabitants*	*3G coverage (% of population)*	*Percentage of households with internet access*	*International internet bandwidth per internet user (kbits/s)*
China	1'004	80	22.9	69.1	98.0	55.5	14.7
India	332	134	1.4	16.8	79.7	22.6	16.0
Brazil	120	66	13	89.5	96.9	52.4	66.2
Russia	88	45	19.4	74.9	75.0	74.8	51.9
South Africa	36	92	2.1	58.6	98.0	53.0	263.0
Germany	67	12	38.8	76.5	96.2	90.8	107.5
United Kingdom	55	5	39.2	91.4	99.6	91.3	66.2
United States	272	16	32.4	124.9	99.9	84.0	126.5

Source: Statista; Statista DMO@2 Statista 2018, ITU Estimates (2017) https://www.itu.int/en/ITU-D/Statistics/Documents/publications/misr2017/MISR2017_Volume2.pdf

Table 5.2: Digital economy size, selected countries, 2016

	Size of Digital Economy (USD trillion)	Share in GDP (as %)
Brazil	0.3754	20.9
China	3.4009	30.3
France	0.962	39
Germany	2.0561	59.3
India	0.4033	17.8
Indonesia	0.1027	11
Japan	2.2935	46.4
Korea	0.6122	43.4
Russia	0.2205	17.2
United Kingdom	1.5358	58.6
United States	10.8318	58.3

Source: OECD Economic Surveys 2019.
https://www.oecd-ilibrary.org/economics/oecd-economic-surveys-china-2019_eco_surveys-chn-2019-en

It is interesting to note that while China's digital economy was still only 32% of the size of the U.S's digital economy in 2016, its annual growth rate was close to 19%, more than three times that of the U.S.', which was around 6%. The digital economy has contributed to nearly 60% of China's GDP growth in 2016 and has emerged as the new driver of economic growth

(ChinaInfo100). Following the expansion of its digital economy, China has emerged as a global leader in several digital services like e-commerce, digital payments, among others.

Table 5.3: Delivered and operational stock of robots used in manufacturing and all industries, selected countries, 2010–2016

		Manufacturing		*All Industries*		*Robot Density in 2016*
		2010	*2016*	*2010*	*2016*	
United States	Delivered Robots	12'746	29'400	16'356	31'404	189
	Operational Stock	96'826	223'105	173'174	250'479	
Germany	Delivered Robots	12'165	16'870	14'061	20'039	309
	Operational Stock	136'939	161'265	148'256	189'270	
United Kingdom	Delivered Robots	845	1'455	878	1'787	71
	Operational Stock	12'335	16'845	13'519	18'471	
China	Delivered Robots	13'008	76'636	14'978	87'000	68
	Operational Stock	26'578	282'807	52'290	339'970	
Thailand	Delivered Robots	966	2'049	2'450	2'646	45
	Operational Stock	2'660	16'951	9'635	28'182	
Malaysia	Delivered Robots	483	1'786	677	1'881	34
	Operational Stock	1'181	5'717	3'677	8'168	
South Africa	Delivered Robots	72	780	213	805	28
	Operational Stock	767	2'895	2'074	4'322	
Brazil	Delivered Robots	595	937	640	1'207	10
	Operational Stock	3'283	10'121	5'721	11'732	
Indonesia	Delivered Robots	191	954	357	964	5
	Operational Stock	387	4'162	1'285	7'155	
India	Delivered Robots	215	2'284	776	2'627	3
	Operational Stock	1'517	11'237	4'855	16'026	
Russian Federation	Delivered Robots	170	144	232	358	3
	Operational Stock	731	2'607	1'058	3'366	

Source: IFR, 2018.

The growth of the digital economy was accompanied by a strong push by China to its research and development activities and innovations. In terms of research output, the Association for the Advancement of Artificial Intelligence (AAAI) indicated a 13% growth in China's research output from 2012 to 2017 compared to a 6% decline in the US. China surpassed the US in terms of delivered and operational stock of robots in 2016 (Table 5.3). While robot density was still lower in China than in the US, delivered robots and the operational stock were much higher in China as compared to any other country, both in the manufacturing sector as well as in all industries.

The main driver of China's digital economy growth has been its comprehensive policy towards building a digital economy. The following section details some of the policies adopted by China to provide a big push to the growth of its digital economy.

5.3 Comprehensive Policy for Digital Transformation

The success of China's digital transformation can be explained by its comprehensive digital policy. This policy was succesfully implemented in three phases which catered to both the demand and supply sides of the digital economy. In phase 1, there was a big push to build network infrastructure, followed by phase 2 with efforts to accelerate deep integration of the internet with the real economy (Figure 5.1). Phase 3 focused on enhancing information technology capabilities in all respects to drive national modernization. Sector-specific policies were also implemented to enhance the digitalization of the sectors.

Figure 5.1: China's Comprehensive Policy for Digital Transformation

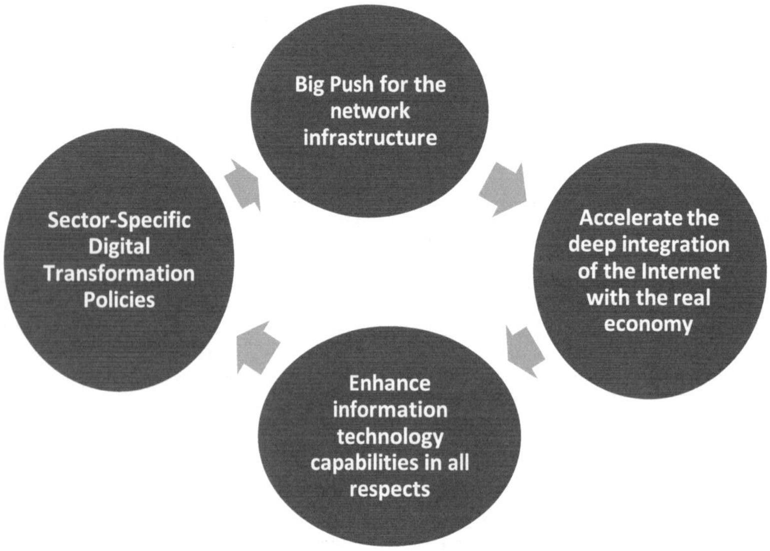

Source: Author's graphical elaboration based on He & Sun (2020).

5.3.1 Big Push for Network Infrastructure

To develop its digital infrastructure, the Chinese Government launched a national strategy, i.e., ***Broadband China Strategy and Its Implementation Plan*** in August 2013. This strategy outlined the technical roadmap, development timetable, and main tasks for speeding up broadband network construction. He and Sun (2020) outline the details of this strategy: [34] Phase 1 included promoting coordinated regional development of broadband networks, accelerating, optimizing and upgrading the broadband networks, improving the level of

[34] https://unctad.org/en/PublicationsLibrary/BRI-Project_RP2_en.pdf

broadband networks application, improving the industrial chain of broadband networks, and building the network security capabilities of broadband networks.

5.3.2 Accelerating the Deep Integration of the Internet with the Real Economy

Phase 2 was implemented in 2015 through the ***Guiding Opinions on Actively Promoting the Internet Plus Action Plan,*** which strategized the expansion of the internet from the consumption sector to the production sector to accelerate industrial upgrading and industrial innovation capability. There were 11 specific actions outlined for urgent digital transformation and upgrading of the real sector, including supporting entrepreneurship and innovation; smart manufacturing and mass customization; modern agricultural systems; smart energy production and consumption; cloud service platforms for internet finance; internet-based public services; smart logistics and warehousing; rural, industrial and cross-border e-commerce; internet-based transportation infrastructure; and use of artificial intelligence

5.3.3 Enhancing Information Technology Capacities

The third phase started in 2016 when the Chinese Government published the ***Outline of National Information Technology Development Strategy,*** which guided the information technology development for the next decade and emphasized building technology capacities. Five measures were suggested, including developing core technologies, consolidating infrastructure, taping information resources, upgrading talent teams, and deepening cooperation and exchanges.

5.3.4 Identifying Priorities Areas for Digital Transformation in the Future

(a) Services

China has also adopted sector-specific policies to increase both demand and supply in the digital economy. To boost the demand in the digital economy, the digital transformation of various services sectors has been the focus of the policy. In this respect, in 2013, the *Several Opinions on Promoting Information Consumption to Expand Domestic Demand* was published, which targeted boosting information consumption at the national level. Accordingly, the information infrastructure was developed, including broadband coverage, speed, and price. In August 2017, the *Guiding Opinions on Further Expanding and Upgrading Information Consumption to Constantly Release the Potential of Domestic Demand* was issued, which again provided policy support for information consumption. As an upgraded version, Information Consumption 2.0 identified priorities areas which included *Life-related information consumption,* ***Public service-related information consumption, Industry-related information consumption and New types of information consumption*** like novel information products such as virtual reality, augmented reality, intelligent and connected vehicles, and intelligent service robots.

(b) Industry

The Chinese digital policies included the long-term strategic task of promoting deep integration of informatization and industrialization. In line with this, they published the *Special Plan of Action on Deep Integration of Informationization and Industrialization (2013–2018)* and *Implement the Guiding Opinions on Actively Promoting the Internet Plus Action Plan (2015–2018)*, which continuously deepens the understanding and steps up the effort in the integration of industry with the information economy. Focusing on the manufacturing sector, the Chinese Government issued the *Guiding Opinions on Deepening the Integration of Manufacturing and Internet* in 2016, which provided a guide for systematically deepening the integration of manufacturing and Internet. This was done through entrepreneurship and innovation platforms, new models, new formats and new ecosystems.

To achieve the above objectives by 2050, China traced a development trajectory, which plans that:

- **By 2025,** an infrastructure and industrial systems with international competitiveness will be created. Three to five global Internet platforms up to international standards will be created, and one million industrial APPs and millions of enterprise clouds will be cultivated.
- **By 2035,** the world's leading industrial Internet infrastructure and platform will be put in place.
- **By 2050,** the industrial Internet infrastructure will fully support economic and social development. The industrial Internet will reach international advanced levels in terms of innovation capability, technological and industrial system, integration and application, and rank front in comprehensive strength.

(c) Agriculture

To bridge the rural-urban digital divide and deepen the internet economy and agriculture integration, the Chinese government has developed a long-term plan with immediate implementation. A comprehensive digital blueprint was developed for agriculture focusing on advancing the modernization of agriculture. In 2018, the *Opinions on Implementing the Strategy of Rural Revitalization* prioritized speeding up the coverage of broadband networks and 4G mobile communication networks in rural areas. Further, this strategy focused on developing information technologies, products, applications, and services adapted to the characteristics of agriculture, rural areas and farmers. Finally, it pushes forward the popularization of telemedicine, distance education, and similar applications. In May 2019, the *Outline of Digital Countryside Development Strategy* was officially unveiled. Based on field investigations, opinions, and suggestions from stakeholders, it focused on the overarching design and overall planning for digital countryside construction. Four stages were identified:

- **By 2020,** initial progress will be made in digital countryside construction and rural penetration rate.
- **By 2025,** major progress will be made in digital countryside construction, with the urban-rural digital divide effectively narrowed. 5G innovations will be gradually applied while 4G gains more popularity in the countryside. The rural cyberculture will prosper from more convenient circulation services, and the rural digital governance system will be in place.
- **By 2035,** substantial progress will be made in digital countryside construction. The digital divide between urban and rural areas will be sharply reduced and the digital literacy of farmers will be significantly improved. In addition to the modernization of agricultural and rural areas, the equalization of basic public services in urban and rural areas and the modernization of rural governance system and capacity will be prioritized.
- **By 2050,** the digital countryside will be built in all respects to support full rural revitalization with strong agriculture and rich farmers.

(c) Successful Implementation of the Comprehensive Digital Policy

It is important to note that China's comprehensive digital policy was successfully implemented, as Figure 2 highlights some indicators. They include rapid growth of broadband penetration, a steep rise in fixed broadband speed, and a steady decline in broadband tariffs.

Figure 5.2: Indicators of Successful Implementation of China's Comprehensive Digital Policy

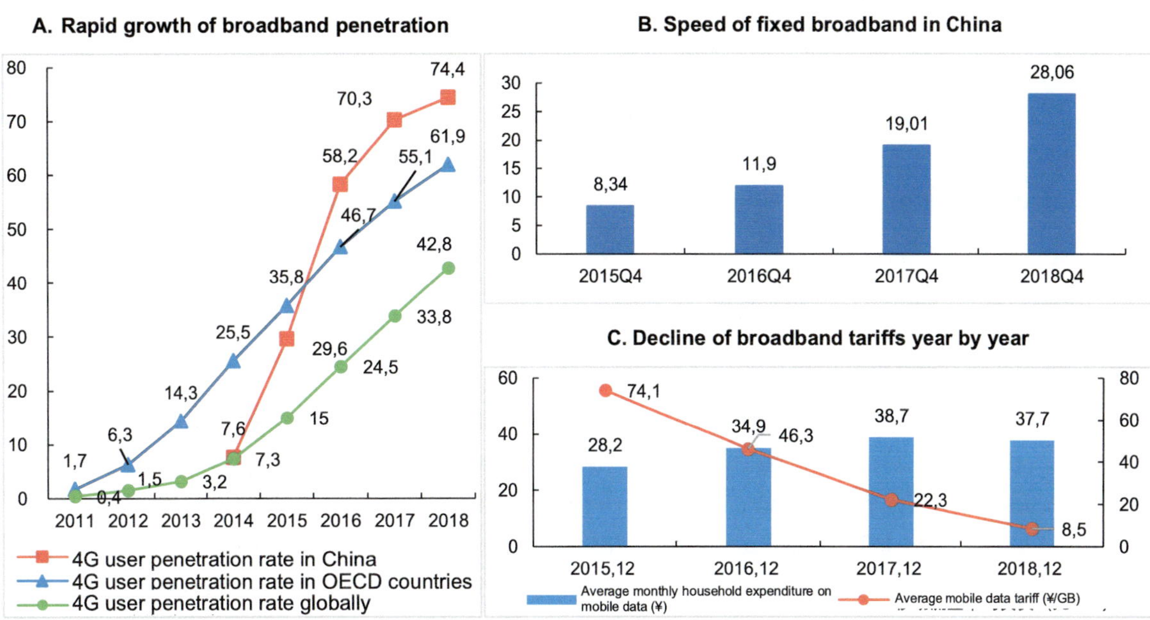

Source: He & Sun (2020).

Along with these successes, the broadband infrastructure was strengthened in all the 31 provinces in the country. Each of them released plans or opinions for implementing the Broadband China Strategy and upgrading the broadband development. Cloud computing infrastructure was also strengthened and a *Three-Year Action Plan for Cloud Computing Development (2017–2019)* initiated a series of measures for its development and application.

Further, China has also concentrated on building data centres for storing and processing data. By the end of 2017, China had built 125 large and super-large data centres. The western region accommodated an increasing proportion of data centres that widely used green and energy-saving technologies. Cloud computing was enabled in 24% of data centres, and industrial clusters were taking shape.

To achieve the objectives outlined by the comprehensive digital policy, China scrapped domestic roaming charges by mobile operators in July 2018. The average internet speed in China has increased to 16 Mbps (CNNIC, 2018b for Q3 2017), double the world average. By the end of 2017, all cities in China were covered by fibre-optic networks, with a penetration rate of 84 per cent. Further, China has become the world's largest telecommunication market in terms of mobile number, fixed-telephone, fixed-broadband, mobile broadband subscriptions, and exports of ICT products.

China's policy implementation became so successful that by the end of 2018, the FTTH (Fiber-to-the-home) penetration in administrative villages hit 98%, and the broadband penetration in poverty-stricken villages exceeded 97%, which means that the 13th Five-Year Plan objective of providing over 90% coverage was achieved ahead of schedule.

5.4 Comprehensive Digital Policy for Developing E-Commerce Sector

The e-commerce sector growth in China is exemplary for the world. According to the annual *E-commerce in China* reports by China's Ministry of Commerce, online retail sales in China reached over 1.3 trillion USD in 2018. They accounted for 18.4% of the whole retail sales in China and 46.64% of global online retail sales.[35] Several super digital platforms like Alibaba have emerged in China, giving tough competition to the existing e-commerce platforms like Amazon.

5.4.1 Rise of Alibaba

Alibaba was founded in June 1999 and started as an online business-to-business (B2B) marketplace. It assisted small and medium-sized enterprises to find overseas trading partners. With a decade, Alibaba rose from a B2B marketplace to a digital giant, and by 2019, Alibaba Group had their own B2B, B2C (business-to-consumer) and C2C (consumer-to-consumer) online retailing platforms. It had established its own payment and credit system (Alipay) and a logistic system with some partners. It also now provides cloud computing and big data consulting services. In China, Alibaba also outcompeted both eBay and Amazon, which shut their Chinese business in 2006 and 2019, respectively.

---

[35] http://dzsws.mofcom.gov.cn/article/ztxx/ndbg/

The rise of Alibaba can be attributed to both its successful business model as well as the digital eco-system created by the government to facilitate the growth of enterprises. One of the biggest challenges faced by Alibaba was the serious trust issues between sellers and buyers. To address these trust issues, in 2004, Alibaba introduced Alipay, an innovative digital payment method. Alipay created an escrow account to eliminate the settlement risk. When buyers submitted their payments, the money went to the Alipay escrow account and not directly to the sellers. After the buyers received the products and found the products satisfactory, they asked Alipay to release the money to the sellers. This system was substantially different from the direct payment method offered by foreign digital platforms. Buyers on eBay submitted their payment via Pay pal directly to the sellers, which could not alleviate trust concerns in online transactions.

With mobile internet development, Alibaba further promoted Alipay mobile payment with its QR code payment method to offline merchants ranging from supermarkets and restaurants to taxis and theme parks. Additionally, Alibaba launched **Ali Wangwang instant message** service to allow buyers to interact with sellers directly. Unlike eBay's commission-based business model, Alibaba did not charge listing fees and commissions for sellers. Its revenue was mainly from data-driven search keyword auctions for sellers. With millions of users' transaction data and trillions of RMB payments on Alipay accounts, Alibaba launched the AliLoan microfinance service in 2010. By analyzing the merchant's transaction record data, Alibaba could issue loans up to 1 million RMB to small or mid-size merchants within hours without requiring collateral.

To facilitate the logistics of its supplies, in 2013, **Alibaba founded Cainiao Logistics** (Cainiao) jointly with five leading logistics companies in China. It is a **data-driven intelligent logistic service** that handles inventory and parcel deliveries for millions of third-party merchants on Alibaba. By analyzing the data from orders in every step of the logistics chain, Cainiao significantly increased the efficiency for logistics firms and improved users' shopping experiences on Alibaba. Alibaba launched its cloud computing service, **Alibaba Cloud**, in 2009. Now, it ranks as the first cloud service provider in China and the third in the world, only after Amazon's AWS and Microsoft's Azure.

Alibaba's rise as a digital super-platform shows that data analytics and infrastructure are the key drivers of the E-commerce business.

5.4.2 Next Alibaba

A national mass entrepreneurship and innovation campaign has been launched to encourage the emergence of more entrepreneurs and promote the top-down culture shift. This culture attracts an unprecedented number of talents from big companies overseas, colleges, and venture capital funds to build *Next Alibaba*. The total Chinese venture capital funds skyrocketed from around 3 billion USD in 2013 to 12 billion USD in 2014 and 26 billion USD in 2015.

5.5. China's Data Governance Policies and Regulations

Data is the crucial element driving the digital economy. China understood the importance of data and has put in place appropriate data governance policies and regulations that have helped China developing its digital competitiveness. China has established a legal system for its data protection, including the *Criminal Law, General Principles of Civil Law, Cyber Security Law, E-commerce Law, Law on the Protection of Consumer Rights and Interests*, and *Regulations on the Protection of Personal Information of Telecommunications and Internet Users*.

5.5.1 Data Security, Data Localization and Promoting Big Data Analytics

To maintain data security, ***the Cyber Security Law*** stipulates which data shall be stored within China's territory, including personal information and important data collected and generated in domestic operations of critical information infrastructure. In case such data are transferred across borders for business needs, security assessments shall be conducted.

Attaching importance to national data sovereignty, China encourages data localization. It stipulates that the data generated by important fields involving national security and public interest are required to be stored in China. For example, The *Regulations on the Administration of Credit Investigation* provided that the collection, storage, and processing of information collected by credit investigation agencies within China shall be conducted within China's territory. Further, the *Regulations on Map Management* requires Internet map service agencies to set up servers for map data storage in China's territory and develop data security management systems and safeguard measures for Internet maps.

The importance of developing Big data and promoting its application the *Action Outline for Promoting the Development of Big Data* was issued in 2015. It pointed out that by promoting the development of big data, China will accelerate the construction of national data strength and release technological, institutional, and innovation dividends. Further, three specific tasks were set down: accelerating governance data openness and sharing to improve governance capacity; encouraging industrial innovation to catalyze economic transition; and strengthening data security for healthy development".

5.5.2 Inclusive and Prudent Regulation

A vital approach adopted by the Chinese government in building its data infrastructure and digital ecosystem has been to adopt inclusive and prudent regulations. This approach implies that, in the beginning, the government gave complete freedom to the internet businesses and innovators to develop it without any regulations and restrictions. This concept emphasizes the role of policy space needed by developing countries to cultivate their digital ecosystems.

5.5.3 China's Cross-Border E-Commerce (CBEC) Policies-Exports and Imports

According to the "2016-2017 China CBEC Market Research Report" released by iResearch, the number of China's CBEC buyers reached 41 million in 2016, with a growth rate of 78%. By 2018, China's CBEC buyers reached 0.74 billion, increasing by an annual compound growth rate of 96%, which greatly exceeds the CBEC (54.1%) and the entire e-commerce industry (31.5%). In terms of import and export ratio, China's CBEC accounted for 83.3% of exports and 16.7% of imports in 2015.

In recent years, to improve the cross-border e-commerce system and strengthen the regulatory mechanism, China has issued a positive and negative list policy on cross-border e-commerce for imports and exports. The government continued its encouraging attitude, increased its support for the industry, created a favourable tax policy environment, and encouraged social capital to invest in the platform exports. On April 8th, 2016, the government implemented tax policies for retailing import of CBEC and adjusted the postal tax policy. In addition, the authorities released a positive list of CBEC retail imports for overseas shopping. On March 17th, 2017, the Ministry of Commerce clarified that it would regulate the CBEC retail imports of personal items.

5.6 Key Policy Lessons from China's Digital Transformation and Way Forward for Developing Countries

While it may not be possible for developing countries to replicate policies that helped China's digital transformation given the country's unique political and economic realities, some key lessons can be drawn from the successful implementation of policies.

- The first and foremost lesson that emerges is that China did not emulate the West when designing its policies for promoting digitalization. Developing countries have unique business models and different challenges as compared to developed countries, which may require different laws and regulations from those set up by the developed countries. Therefore, policies need to take into account the ground realities.
- China realized the importance of building capacities for digitalization much before other developing countries. Accordingly, it started building its ICT infrastructure, focusing on ICT's supply and demand. For this purpose, it started improving people's capability to use ICT as consumers. Simultaneously the government designed policies to connect ICT infrastructure with manufacturing and began training its population to use ICT as producers.
- China well understood the importance of data in the digital world. It, therefore, designed comprehensive data protection policies and regulations on data flow. The government adopted adequate data localization policies to build national capacity for storing data and digital skills for processing data.
- Digital infrastructure, which goes much beyond ICT infrastructure, was slowly but steadily developed in all Chinese provinces with support from the Centre. This infrastructure included broadband and cloud computing.

- Detailed policies were designed to encourage digital innovations and start-ups in all sectors, including agriculture, manufacturing, and services.
- Appropriate e-commerce policies were designed to encourage the growth of digital platforms. Further support was provided to help them grow into super platforms.
- Necessary logistical infrastructure was built along with online payment infrastructure to support the digital economy.

All these policies were a part of a very comprehensive National Digital Policy and were not implemented as ad hoc policies. Coordination between ministries and between different provinces helped in the successful implementation of these policies.

Given the growing digital divide, developing countries need to design national policies which can help their rapid digital transformation. Although it may not be possible to replicate China's digital policies given the existing socio-economic-political differences among developing countries, an important learning from China's comprehensive national digital policy is that digitalization cuts across sectors and, therefore, requires a comprehensive strategy. Strategic interventions are needed in all sectors of the economy to progress in its digital transformation with efforts to build both the demand and the supply sides. Producers need to be digitally empowered with digital technologies, and consumers need to be trained to use digital infrastructure. Labour digital skills need to be improved through advanced training, and digital education needs to be incorporated as early as possible in the schools.

It is also important to be aware of the digital rules discussed or negotiated at the international level. At the same time, it is essential to preserve policy space to be able to design national digital policies required for digital transformation. UNCTAD has proposed a ten-point digital cooperation agenda at the regional level, providing regional support to small developing countries in their digital transformation.[36]

CHAPTER 6

Insights on Debt Sustainability and Management from China's Structural Transformation Experience

Chapter 6: Insights on Debt Sustainability and Management from China's Structural Transformation Experience

6.1 Introduction and Context[37]

China has engaged in rapid transformation lifting millions out of poverty and has become an economic superpower, all the while avoiding unsustainable sovereign debt. From the perspective of debt, China's exceptionalism emerges in several ways: the classification of non-financial corporate debt, the growth of productive investment relative to corporate debt, and the ownership of debt. This chapter highlights some of the unique features of China's approach to debt during the last four decades and derives lessons for other developing countries.

With respect to the non-financial corporate debt, comparing the composition of debt stocks for selected countries we find that the share of debt of China's non-financial sector is significant, at just over 61 per cent of its debt stocks in 2019 (Figure 6.1).

While such a large share of the non-financial debt was also observed in the Russian and Turkish cases, China is unusual in that a significant part of this debt - perhaps 20% or more - includes urban construction-related debt held by local government investment vehicles and SOEs (Herrero, 2020). In most other countries, this share of the debt would be reflected as central government debt. This accounts for what is often termed as China's "off-balance-sheet" deficit.

A second remarkable difference is that contrary to other developing countries, in China, taken as a whole, the proliferation of corporate indebtedness has not outgrown productive investment. Although, as the recent example of Evergrande reveals (FT, 2021), highly indebted non-financial corporations and non-financial private sector are not immune to a severe deleveraging process in the future. Instead, the growth rate of non-financial corporate debt far exceeds the growth rate of private capital stock (TDR, 2019). This needs to be seen in the context of the explosion of financial innovation since the late 1980s, leading ultimately to collapse known as the Global Financial Crisis (GFC). The financial innovation during this time was largely directed towards complex financial instruments related to securitized mortgages, commodities futures, and a range of other financial derivatives rather than productive investments (Mazzucato and Wray, 2015).

[37] This chapter is prepared by Penelope Hawkins based on the paper prepared by Zhang and Lu (2020), "Debt Sustainability and Debt Management: Lessons from China" available at https://unctad.org/system/files/official-document/BRI-Project_RP5_en.pdf

Figure 6.1: Composition of debt stocks, selected countries, 2019

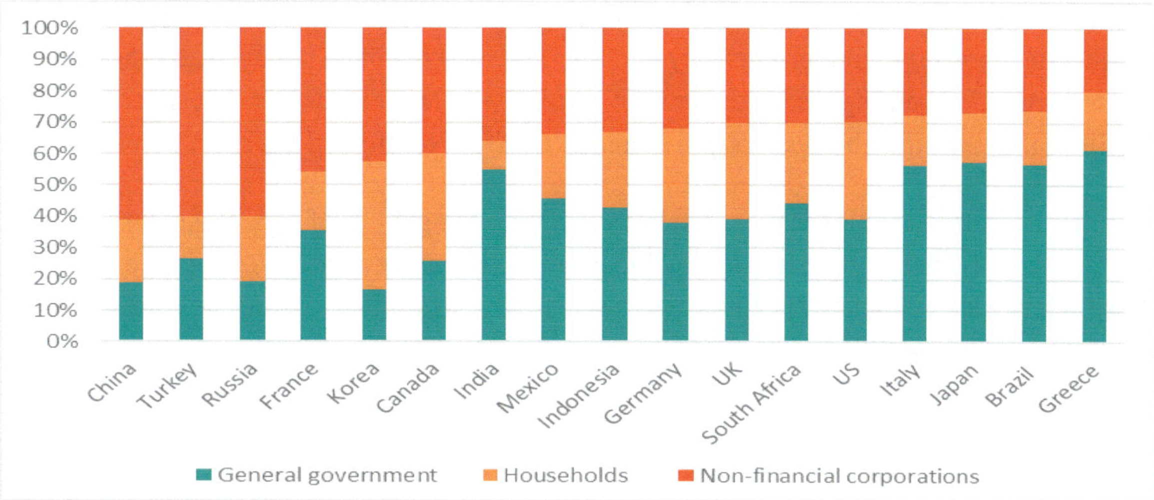

Source: Bank for international settlements.

Figure 6.2: Growth rates of private corporate debt and private capital stock, selected developing countries, 2008–2015

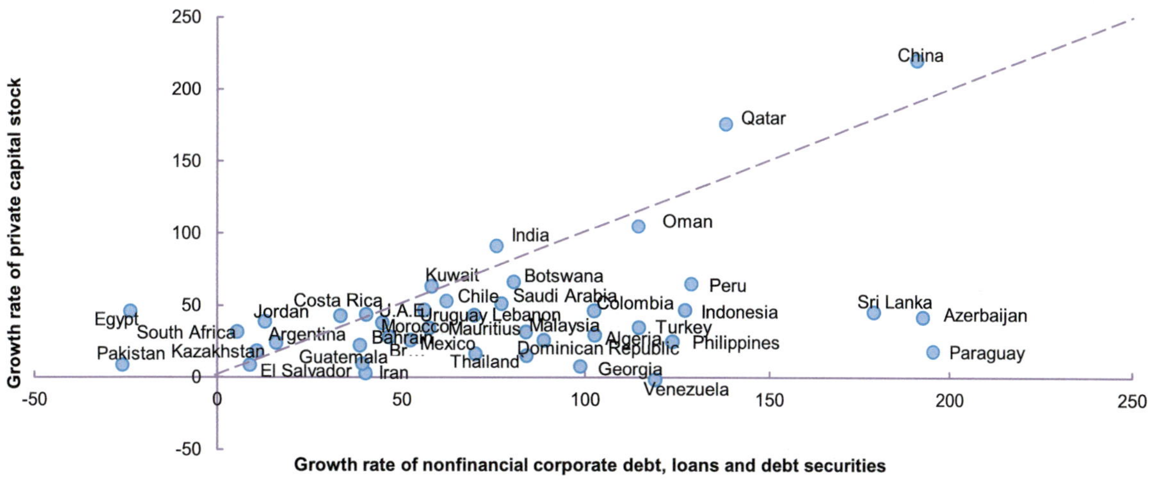

Source: UNCTAD secretariat calculations based on IMF Global Debt Database and IMF Investment and Capital Stock Data.

This tendency is reflected in Figure 6.2, where between 2008 and 2015 non-financial corporate debt grew considerably faster than investment in physical capital stock in most developing countries for which such data are available (depicted by all observations situated below the 45-degree line in the figure). In China, non-financial corporate debt has been channelled by local governments into what is assumed to be fiscally sustainable infrastructure investment. While it is true that some local governments are heavily indebted and over-invested in a few sectors, their infrastructure investment is likely to lift growth over the medium to longer term. Moreover, this indebtedness is currently not providing an external constraint to the country (see section 6.3).

Regarding external constraints and vulnerabilities, it is worth noting that both the ownership and currency of China's debt are predominantly domestic. The denomination in domestic currency is particularly important in China's case as infrastructure investment typically does not generate revenues in foreign currency in the short term – although it may enable subsequent export activity. Accruing debt in domestic currency is an advantage when it is used for activities other than tradable sectors that generate foreign exchange in the short term.

The role of China's state investment banks in enabling the growth of capital stock relative to debt has provided an effective institutional mechanism to ensure finance for local government infrastructure (see Section 6.2). This role of state investment banks is further emphasised in Mazzucato and Penna (2014).

The very high levels of non-financial corporate debt as a share of total debt, the positive contribution of this debt to the accumulation of capital stock growth, and the domestic nature of China's debt provide the point of departure to explore further lessons from China during its structural transformation.

The remaining parts of this chapter are organised as follows: Section 6.2 examines the key policy stances related to China's historical experience; section 6.3 links these policy stances to lessons from China's structural transformation; section 6.4 explores some of the debt statistics and policies of the selected developing countries, namely, Ethiopia, Indonesia, and Sri Lanka and revisits some of China's current policies. Section 6.5 concludes.

6.2 Policies and Experiences from China

This section examines China's debt policy over the past forty years – a period in which the country invested heavily, grew rapidly, and transformed structurally (Sun, 2019). The substantial capital investment undertaken over this time – together with a responsive policy framework - created a virtuous feedback loop within the economy that was undergirded with a particular strategic stance on development finance and debt.

Like many countries, China's acquisition of debt was a tool of structural transformation. However, China's experience in the past four decades has been more successful than most developing countries, exhibiting the fastest growth of all nations between 1995 and 2015. To achieve this, investment funded by predominantly domestic debt was directed by the "Entrepreneurial State"[38] to meet the country's strategic development goals, including towards conglomerate projects that, together, had a higher likelihood of generating future revenue,

---

[38] Burlamaqui (2015, p.45) sees the three core elements of the Entrepreneurial state as a) a banking system that produces finance for productive capital (rather than speculation or financialization), b) an extension to the government, of Schumpeter's link between entrepreneurial skills and structural change, and c) the presence of a robust degree of socialization of investment as stated by Keynes. For Burlamaqui, the Chinese state encapsulates all these elements.

while structuring the debt so that it would not be a burden to the central government. We will explore these in turn.

6.2.1 A Strategic Approach to Debt

China's experience is instructive in showing debt does not necessarily have to pre-empt or disrupt development goals and achievement of structural transformation. Instead, debt sustainability and structural transformation can be mutually reinforcing. China's development is often broadly divided into three periods: from 1953 to 1978, when China prioritized heavy industry through the centrally planned economy; from 1979 to 1999, when the promotion of light industries and decentralized market and private sector activity took place often with the involvement of foreign direct investment encouraged through export processing zones (REF) and from 2000 to the present day which is characterised by the reappearance of heavy industrialization together with more knowledge-intensive sectors.

From mid-1990s investment was directed towards electricity production and transportation sectors resulting in China's engine of production shifting from rural enterprises to urban enterprises. Investment in both the second and third phases involved investment in urban infrastructure, including water resources, environment, and public facilities management - to better serve the modernized society. During the period 1980-2000, for example, China built 184 ports with associated industrial development and urban residence zones - this model is now known as the 'port–industrial park–city' model associated with the district of Shenkou in the bustling commercial city of Shenzhen (Brautigam, 2019).

The central government played a role in selecting development projects that supported structural transformation goals and industrialization, building up competitive advantages of the economy and stimulating productivity growth. The resulting growth, accompanied by the increased demand from both domestic and international markets, provided revenues through taxes and SOE (State-owned enterprises) profits.

6.2.2 Investment for Infrastructure and Financial Returns

Selection of China's development projects was linked to the likelihood of crowding-in economic activity and thus generation of investment returns. A key criterion was regional focus based on an assessment of factor endowments. The Yangtze and Pearl River delta regions, for example, received many development projects given their geographic, natural resource, and labour advantages. The population densities in these areas were relatively high – and were boosted by mass migration into the hundreds of cities located in these territories. Moreover, local entrepreneurship had been culturally fostered for centuries in these centres because of their trading position. State-led investment in these regions facilitated the formation of region-wide industrial supply chains, with the result that the Yangtze and Pearl River delta regions benefited from economies of scale and emerged as the leading economic centres of the country (see Zhang and Lu, 2020).

The nature of infrastructure investment requires a balancing of long and short-term returns. For example, in the case of the ports – which are highly capital intensive, with low rates of return on capital associated with slow depreciation, China gave preference to joint ventures with foreign investors who were expected to provide capital and operating efficiencies (Brautigam, 2019).

6.2.3. Devolution of debt

From 1994, the acquisition of debt was devolved as a central government function to local government, in line with tax distribution reform that reduced local fiscal revenue by 25 per cent. As detailed below, this shift in responsibility for management of the debt (and revenue) was seen by the central authorities as a way of encouraging individual and market incentives and discipline in ensuring careful debt management and returns on investment. From a theoretical view, it can be seen as allowing for "regulated managerial freedom"[39].

The shift to local government responsibility to take on and manage debt was a key departure, since government-backed liabilities, either in the form of direct governmental borrowing or state-owned enterprise debt, had constituted the biggest bulk of the total debt outstanding and prompted most of the economic growth in China to that point. The shift encouraged a more active role by key financial institutions – including both commercial banks and national development banks – in supporting local governments' shortfall in development funding through financial innovations, as well as in the process of project selection and risk management.

6.3 Lessons from China

China capitalized on its large domestic market and central control not only to implement the basic strategy associated with development finance, but pragmatically and flexibly implemented its strategy to ensure debt sustainability. Simply put, the key lesson is that debt should not be regarded as a burden but as a policy instrument.

As mentioned above, well-targeted development investment was a key part of the strategy to ensure debt sustainability. Infrastructure investment that expanded market boundaries and generated revenues by promoting private business activities, including through foreign direct investment, was promoted by China's government, as were projects that could enhance access to global markets. The state's aim was to secure both short and long-run irevenue, laying a solid foundation for fiscally sustainable growth.

To achieve optimized decision-making in investment and financing, China adopted a decentralized economic development structure from 1994. Local officials were assigned with the authority to roll out local economic policies, including financing and launching development projects. Implicit within this approach was that local authorities were better

[39] A key concept in Schumpeter's view of socialist society (see, eg Burlamaqui, 2015).

connected with local enterprises and institutions than the central government, and better equipped to monitor the projects, reducing associated operational and financial risks.

The mechanism which catalysed this shift was the 1994 "Tax-sharing Fiscal Reform", which shifted the responsibility of local economic management to local officials. It provided both positive and negative incentives - the personal status of local officials was linked to GDP-based performance evaluation leading to competition to generate economic growth, while the distribution of central government revenues dried up and retention of local government revenue was massively reduced. The reform instituted the necessity of generating local government revenue.

Simultaneously, local governments were prohibited from generating fiscal deficits or guarantees. The outcome led to a reliance on the Local Government Funding Vehicle (LGFV) mechanism – essentially off-balance sheet structure, into which the assets of infrastructure projects were bundled, to provide collateral necessary to borrow from one of the infrastructure banks[40] - most notably - the China Development Bank (CBD). The bundling of long-term, capital-intensive infrastructure projects – each with diverse cash flow patterns, and varying social benefits, allowed for the smoothing of cash flow. Within a short period, land owned by local governments was leveraged as a principal source of LGFVs' capital, future extra-budgetary revenue, and collateral for LGFV borrowing.

The LGFV financing mechanism was successful in freeing local governments from their financial constraints but the convenience of the mechanism, together with the ambition of local officials, resulted in a significant rise in the local government debt burden. This was accentuated by the massive stimulus initiated by China after the Global Finance Crisis: an infrastructure investment programme amounting to RMB 4.5 trillion (USD 650 billion).[41]

Between 2010 and 2014, local government debt grew by over 20 per cent p.a, and this, together with reliance on land as collateral, increased risks - at the same time contingent liabilities remained obscure. To address transparency and debt, regulations restricting LGFV lenders were imposed in 2010 - leaving only the CBD involved – and by 2014, LGFVs were banned outright. However, by 2016, the off-balance sheet debt associated with LGFVs still amounted to 4,5 per cent of GDP[42]. The central government instead allowed for direct financing through the bond market, with banks, non-financial corporates and the shadow banking sector growing their exposure. Public and Private Partnerships (PPPs) were also promoted as an alternative financing model, although criticized for excessive reliance on short-term debt.

---

[40] The six biggest LGFV lenders between 2008 and 2012 were: China Development Bank (CDB), Industrial and Commercial Bank of China (ICBC), China Construction Bank (CCB), Agricultural Bank of China (ABC), Bank of China (BOC), and Bank of Communications (BoCom). Zhang and Li (2020) refer to CBD as a policy bank and the others as state-owned commercial banks. In addition, there are privately owned commercial banks including China Merchants Bank and Huaxia Bank.

[41] Herrero, 2014.

[42] Herrero, 2020.

From a financing point of view, the relationships between local governments, development banks, and commercial institutions are also instructive. Both state-owned and private commercial banks were involved in raising money for local governments and their development projects, especially during the era of LGFVs. After the prohibition of LGFVs, commercial banks provided comprehensive financial services for PPPs. They established PPP industrial investment funds, issued special bonds for PPPs, and created a trading platform for PPP assets.

Policy banks like CDB played not only the role of finance provision but oversight of infrastructure in alignment with the country's long-term planning. In this way, the policy banks effectively provide a monitoring and internal credit rating system for the local government and its officials. Stabilized by large-scale medium- and long-term bond issuance, policy banks have been able to finance long-term development investment and mitigate the risks on development projects for commercial institutions, enabling them to enter the field of public good provision.

Related to the role of public development banks in China, reliance on domestic, rather than external, debt is notable. Domestic (or internal) financing of government debt, as opposed to foreign borrowing, has a fundamental advantage - namely that domestic borrowing keeps financial resources within the economy. In this view, domestic debt conserves financial resources because the counterpart of the government's liability is the asset held by residents who are owed money by the government. Such government debt requires regular transfers of money from taxpayers to holders of government bonds in the form of interest and agreed repayments. In the case of external debt, the liabilities of a government are assets for foreign residents, and interest and repayments represent transfers from taxpayers in the economy to residents outside the country (Toporowski, 2021). Moreover, the country needs to generate revenues in foreign currency to pay it. As will be seen below, the beneficiary countries of the existing UNCTAD project all have considerably more reliance on external debt than China.

Throughout, the Chinese central government was alert to threats to macroeconomic stability or debt vulnerability. A case in point is its actions relating to the deleveraging of the non-financial corporate sector in recent years (Zhang and Lu, 2019). Following the credit binge of China's non-financial corporate sector in the wake of the post-GFC stimulus package[43], the debt-to-GDP ratio for the sector rose from 95 per cent at the end of 2008 to 158 per cent in 2016, exposing a material threat to the country's debt sustainability and financial stability. China's central government deployed several policy initiatives to curb further rise of corporate debt level, including disciplining state-owned enterprises and LGFVs from over-borrowing, cleaning up a large number of zombie companies[44], forbidding loans to sectors deemed to have

[43] Including LGFVs - registered to circumvent the regulations on local government debt issuance, their debt was categorized as non-financial corporate debt.

[44] At the end of 2016, China launched a three-year program to resolve around 2,000 zombie enterprises that suffered extended losses and had outdated production capacity. Restructuring options including mergers and consolidation, liquidation, debt-equity swaps, and corporate asset sales. By October 2019, more than 95 percent of zombie companies and enterprises had been phased out.

overcapacity, and regulating the shadow banking. Non-financial sector debt as a percentage of GDP peaked in mid-2017 and began to decline until the end of 2018.

A key role of China's central government was to balance economic growth and debt management. In the Chinese case, the condition for stable, sustainable debt is not the size of the stock of debt in relation to the size of the national economy, or the scale of debt servicing in relation to exports or reserves, but capacity to borrow in domestic credit markets and balancing the annual debt servicing cost with taxes on corporate revenue, wealth and financial assets.

A sharp decline in economic growth, for example, is likely to reduce a country's repayment capacity significantly and increase the possibility of a debt constraint even when the absolute volume of the debt stock is shrinking. Managed the way it was, with domestic debt financing and devolution to the LGFVs, China's economic equilibrium and debt sustainability did not require the elimination of fiscal deficits, or avoidance of government debt, but was dealt with by a policy framework that combined fiscal policy with debt management and central bank open market operations and regulation (see Zhang and Lu, 2020). The Chinese experience in this area is clearly not easy to mimic, but there may be aspects that can be applied by developing countries.

In ensuring that debt was employed as an instrument for development, rather than a burden, China's approach provides several lessons to debt sustainability:

(i) Reliance on domestic debt, rather than external debt
(ii) Investment in development projects that can bring in revenues in the short and long run.
(iii) Encouragement of local governments or institutions to take the initiative in development financing and investing.
(iv) Facilitation of development banks and commercial banks to play a role in financing public good provision.
(v) Maintenance of a balance between economic growth and debt accumulation, ensuring that growth is robust enough to ensure sustainable servicing of the debt.

Although each developing country has its specific circumstances, these lessons may be a useful reference point for establishing a strategic approach to debt management for sustainability. In the following section, a brief overview of debt in three developing countries, namely, Ethiopia, Indonesia and Sri Lanka, is presented.

6.4 Overview of External Debt in some Developing Countries

The key difference between the identified developing countries (Ethiopia, Indonesia, and Sri Lanka) and China in terms of debt profile is that China's public debt is largely domestic with public external debt relatively small compared both to domestic debt and to other countries.

Contrary to this, the analysis here focuses largely on the external debt of the countries – for them, this is the greater constraint to development.

Some key debt ratios are set out in Tables 6.1 and 6.2 for the three countries, the average for all developing countries, with and without China, and China itself, for 2019. The data show that China's external debt to GDP is very low at 14.7 percent, pulling the developing country average ratio down (compare all developing countries debt to GDP ratio to all developing countries without China).

Total external debt as a share of GDP is higher in the three countries than the developing country average of 29%, with the two middle-income countries (MICS), Indonesia and Sri Lanka having a higher external debt to GDP ratios at 36 and 67 per cent, respectively. However, given their relatively more robust trade sectors, external debt as a share of exports is lower for Indonesia and Sri Lanka - as compared to Ethiopia – a low-income county (LIC). The levels exceed the developing country average of 110% by some margin. While on average public debt dominates long term external debt for all developing countries, the public debt share is very high in all three beneficiary countries, compared to the developing country averages – with and without China.

Table 6.1: Key debt ratios – 2019

	Total External Debt as % GDP	*Public and publicly guaranteed debt as % of Long-term External debt*	*Private non-guaranteed debt as % of Long-term External debt*	*Total External Debt as % Exports*
Ethiopia	29,4	100,0	0,0	371,8
Indonesia	35,9	65,9	34,1	195,2
Sri Lanka	66,8	80,7	19,3	288,8
Developing country average	29,0	52,0	48,0	110,0
Developing countries without China	38,0	54,0	46,0	127,0
China	14,7	35,4	64,6	80,0

Source: IMF and UNCTAD.

The data in Table 6.2 provide a few additional insights on the ability to service the debt – affordability as measured by such proxies as debt service to export revenue and debt service on PPG debt as a share of government revenue. These ratios show lower affordability for the three beneficiary countries than for all developing countries average. The data show that Indonesia has the highest debt servicing cost relative to export revenue, at nearly 40 per cent, but that Sri Lanka has the highest debt service costs on public debt as a share of government revenue, at nearly 50%. This is a crippling burden for a developing country.

Table 6.2: Key debt ratios - debt servicing and reserves - 2019

2019	*Total Debt Service as % Exports*	*Debt Service on PPG Debt as % Government Revenue*	*Reserves as % Short-term debt*
Ethiopia	29,2	18,2	623,9
Indonesia	39,7	13,3	288,4
Sri Lanka	32,1	46,8	90,6
Developing country average	14,6	4,7	278,0
Developing countries without China	16,7	8,7	292,0
China	10,4	0,7	267,4

Source: IMF and UNCTAD.

Reserves, expressed as a per cent of short-term debt, are very high for Ethiopia at over 6 times the value of the short-term debt, expressing a high precautionary motive, compared to the average developing countries and for the other two beneficiary countries. To the extent that this reserve ratio can be seen as a country's capacity to self-insure against macroeconomic shocks, Sri Lanka's situation is relatively precarious as reserves are less than the short-term external debt exposure in 2019.

Even though Sri Lanka, on balance, faces the most vulnerable situation regarding debt sustainability, it has not been included in the G20's Debt Service Suspension Initiative (DSSI) introduced in April 2020 as a response to the global health, trade, and economic shock emanating from the COVID-19 pandemic. Indonesia, recently declared an upper-middle-income country based on its gross national income (GNI) per capita of US$4,050 in 2019 - above the World Bank upper-middle-income threshold of $3,840, is also excluded. Ethiopia, however, is a beneficiary of the process. While the DSSI was broadly welcomed, it was clear from the outset that it provided only temporary relief relating to postponing repayment of bilateral official debt. As such it is too small a relief for developing countries. In particular, the provision that allowed private creditors and multilateral institutions voluntary participation in the scheme has resulted in a large share of external debt being excluded from this relief, as no voluntary participation has been registered.

This is in spite of the Institute of International Finance (IIF) indicating interest by its members, but a lack of formal applications from beneficiary countries (IIF, 2020). Without private creditors, the full extent of the expected relief during 2020 provided by the G20 initiative for some 43 countries is around US$ 5 billion as at end of September 2020 (US Treasury, 2020). While the individual country benefits of the DSSI have not been published, Ethiopian public debt is largely bilateral official debt, within the scope of the DSSI.

This is not the first time Ethiopia has benefitted from such a scheme: Ethiopia was a HIPC (Highly Indebted Poor Country) and a beneficiary of the Multilateral Debt Relief Initiative (MDRI). These processes started in 1996 with HIPC and culminated in 2005 with the

Multilateral Debt Relief Initiative (MDRI) when it became clear that the HIPC initiative alone would be insufficient to restore long-term debt sustainability in eligible countries and achieve the Millennium Development Goals. As was expected of beneficiaries of the HIPC and MDRI, Ethiopia's debt burden began once again to increase in 2009 with external debt rising to USD 26 billion by June 2018, and USD 28 billion by the end of 2019. Total debt (domestic and external) amounted to USD 49,3 billion, around 49 per cent of GDP (Ethiopian Ministry of Finance, 2018). Taken alone, external debt to GDP amounted to 29% at the end of 2019. The data in Figure 6.3 (and Table 6.1) shows that virtually all of Ethiopia's external debt is long-term debt and all the long-term debt is public debt.

Figure 6.3: External debt stocks (in billions of US Dollars) and short-term debt share (in percent; right scale), Ethiopia, 2000–2018

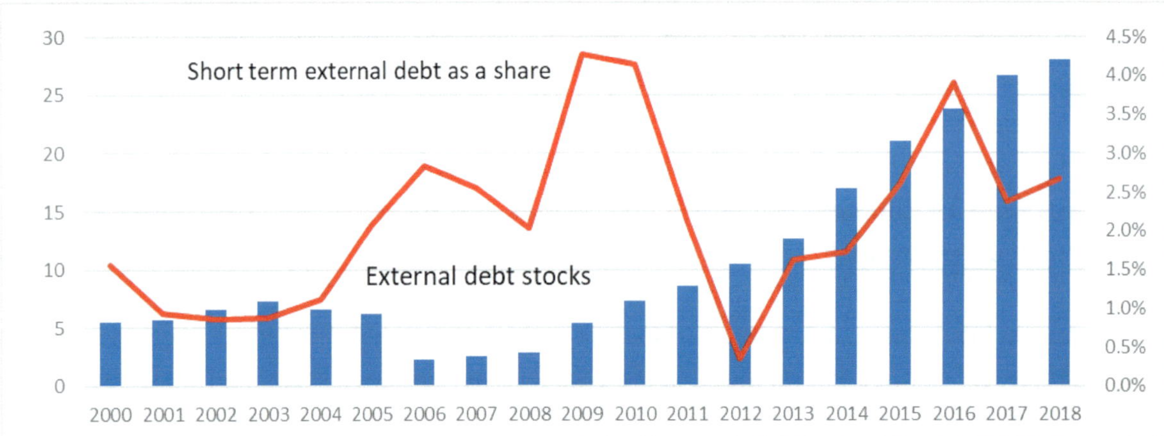

Source: IMF and UNCTAD.

Indonesia's total debt stocks rose above USD 150 billion for the first time in 2008, after the GFC. Since then, it has increased annually so that by 2019, the debt stocks had risen to USD 400 billion. Short-term debt has been a significant share of total debt stocks for some time – although it has never risen above 20% of external debt – see Figure 6.4 (right axis). It fell below 15% in 2015 and has not risen above this level since.

Sri Lanka's exposure to external short-term debt grew from just under 6 per cent of total external debt in 2006 to 18 per cent in 2009, while this fell back in 2010, by 2015, the short-term share accounted for 15,5 per cent in 2018. The total outstanding external debt stock continued to grow in 2019, primarily accounted for by an increase in public debt. The total outstanding external debt to GDP ratio was 66,6 per cent in 2019, from 59,2 per cent of the GDP at the end of 2018, a consequence both of external debt growing and slower nominal GDP growth (Central bank of Sri Lanka, 2020).

Figure 6.4: External debt stocks (in billions of US Dollars) and short-term debt share (in percent; right scale), Indonesia, 2000–2018

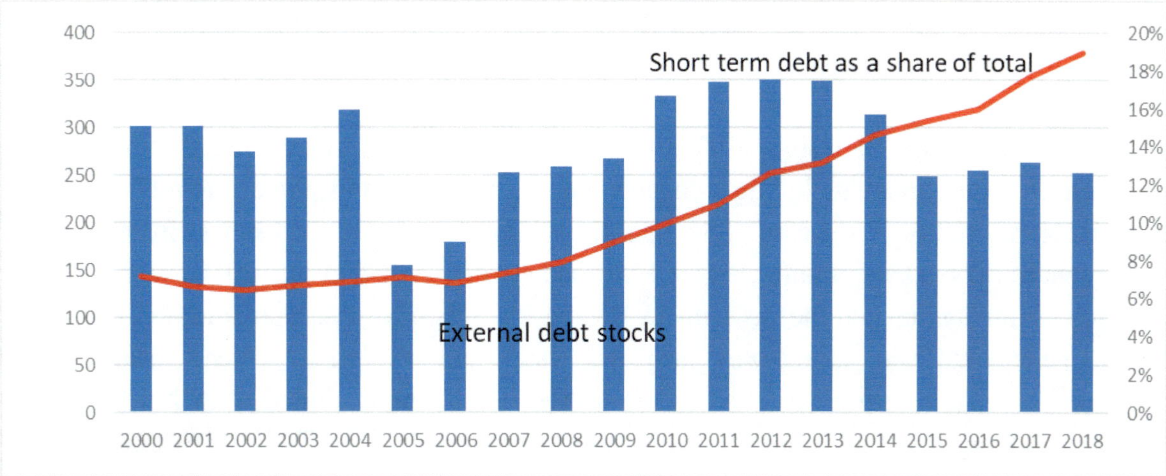

Source: IMF and UNCTAD.

Figure 6.5: External debt stocks (US Dollars) and short-term debt share (in percent; right scale), Sri Lanka, 2000–2019

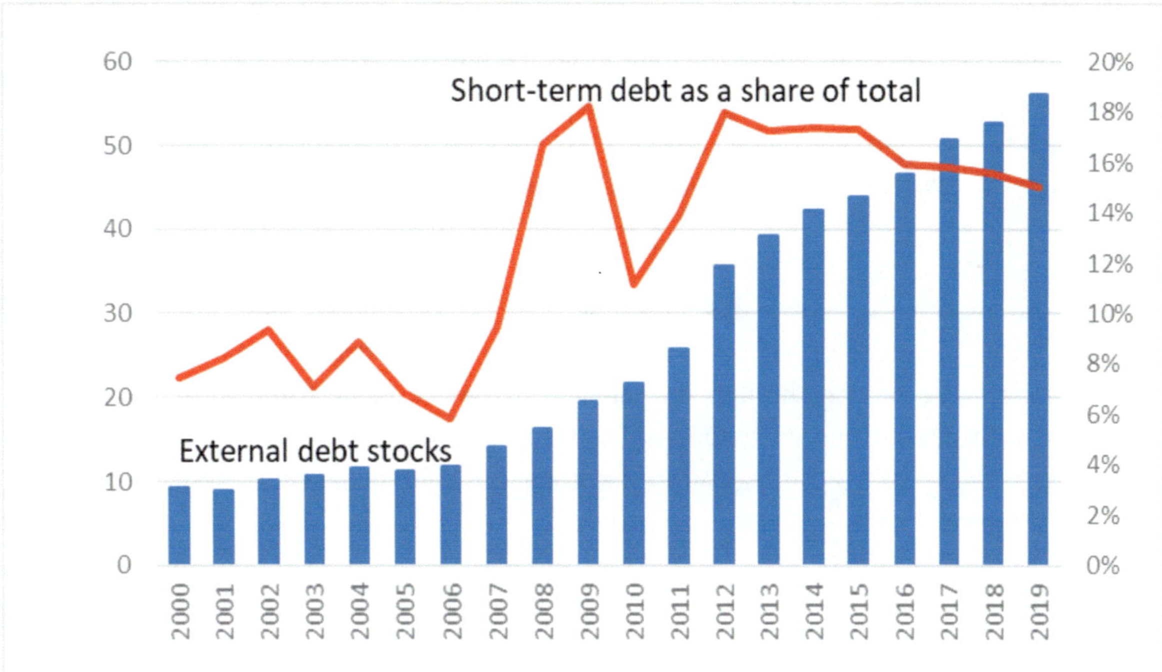

Source: IMF and UNCTAD.

In particular, the outstanding debt position attributed to the central government rose to 63,3 per cent from 61 per cent at the end of 2018, with the total central government debt of Sri Lanka rising to 86,8 per cent of GDP by 2019 (from 78,5 per cent in 2015). Central government revenue fell 12,6 per cent of GDP in 2019, down from 13,4 per cent in 2018. Sri Lanka's tax revenue to GDP ratio is one of the lowest in the world (Central bank of Sri Lanka, 2020).

Finally, a review of the external debt of the three beneficiary countries requires some comment on the loans received as part of China's Belt and Road initiative (BRI). The quantum of the loans extended through the BRI is large, but it should be remembered that as these loans have generally been serviced, this does not equate to debt. In almost all cases, the loans have been for infrastructure investment.

As a recipient of the BRI since 2006, Ethiopia has borrowed some US$13,7 billion for infrastructure investment including transport, communication, and power, as well as water (John Hopkins, 2020). In the case of Sri Lanka, the cumulative value of Chinese infrastructure investment to Sri Lanka amounted to $12.1 billion between 2006 and July 2019 (Wignaraja, et al 2020). China announced the Sri Lankan BRI in 2013, resulting in the Colombo Port City development, road and expressway projects, water and sanitation projects, and further investments in existing projects such as the revised Hambantota Port deal in 2017. Studies show that although Sri Lanka has relatively high external debt, only 6% of its external debt is attributed to China (Wignararja, et al., 2020).

6.5 Conclusions

Sovereign external debt of the three beneficiary countries has grown in recent decades, a trend that is visible across both developing and developed countries alike. This has much to do with hungry capital seeking returns in an era of unprecedented liquidity, together with the high levels of dependency of developing countries on external debt, given their relatively undeveloped capital markets and other financial institutions. The outcome has been growing debt burdens at a time when the pandemic has demanded fiscal space to address health, economic, and trade crises.

The Chinese experience shows that debt can play a constructive and strategic role in development. The process of strategic use of debt in development projects by an entrepreneurial state, acting through its public development banks and local government authorities, provides lessons on mobilising and empowering finance for development, the importance of timeous financial regulation, and enhanced debt management systems.

CHAPTER 7
Conclusions

Chapter 7: Conclusions

7.1 Introduction

The onset of Covid-19 pandemic has multiplied the severity of challenges which developing countries face. The subsequent contraction of the global economy is leading to mass unemployment, with millions of people forced into extreme poverty. While advanced economies are spending billions of dollars as stimulus packages, developing countries with limited financial resources are compelled to revisit their macroeconomic, financial, trade, and industrial policies. The rising debt levels and the widening digital divide create further difficulties for economic recovery in the Global South. The structural transformation of their economies has become necessary to 'recover better' with equitable and resilient growth.

In this context, the book provides an important way forward for the developing countries by sharing policy experiences of China, which is one of the few developing countries which has been able to transform itself from an agrarian economy in the 1980s into a global manufacturing hub in the 1990s and further into a digital leader in the 2000s. The policies followed by China helped its transformation in the areas of macroeconomic, finance, industry, trade, digital economy, and debt sustainability. This book discusses all these topics and brings useful policy lessons that can be drawn for developing countries. While recognizing that developing countries face very different starting points compared to China, it is necessary to emphasize that developing countries should adapt China's policies to their realities. Otherwise, the implementation of the policies may not be as effective. Some of the critical policy lessons which emerge from the analyses in this book are as follows:

7.2 Lessons from China's Macroeconomic and Financial Policies

Three essential lessons emerge from China's macroeconomic and financial policy experience. *First,* developing countries should maintain a flexible macroeconomic framework that can adapt and respond to changing needs and circumstances. Developing countries need this flexibility to react to business cycles that emerge at the core of the global economic system. Further, they also have narrower economic structures, making them more susceptible to macroeconomic volatility and external shocks. China's flexible fiscal and monetary policies combined with a cautious approach to capital account liberalization helped minimize major adverse impacts from external shocks, which often derive from massive capital inflows and outflows. China's policy experience in this area also highlights that no fixed formula for rapid catch-up and development exists. It is a process of trial and error, so developing countries should not hesitate to readjust their policies when faced with failures.

Second, as seen in the case of China, public investments can be a vital tool to trigger a virtuous growth process, which can help in the transformation process of the developing countries. Public investments can also be used as a counter-cyclical tool to stimulate the economy in times of faltering demand. Private investments can be crowded-in by public investments, especially when domestic demand is weak and world trade lacks traction. Public investments can also set expenditure priorities along with social and environmental targets for long-term sustainable growth. It can also play an essential role in creating fiscal space, i.e., by stimulating aggregate demand with subsequent growth and tax revenue expansion that is a by-product of growth itself. In addition, public investment can be used to target bottlenecks, thereby creating new space for pro-growth policies.

Third, China's policy experience shows that financial institutions can play a key role in accelerating growth. In China, development banks played a critical role in supporting public and private enterprises, urban sector development, development of the agricultural sector, renovation of old industries and shift towards new industries and green development. These development banks need to operate with the support of the central bank and other financial institutions, which must provide large-scale funding required to finance the banks' operations in multiple areas for transformative growth.

7.3 Lessons from China's Industrial Policy

China's successful transformation from an agrarian economy to a global manufacturing hub can provide important insights for developing countries regarding industrial policy design. Two general principles have guided China's industrial policies. The first one is the process of testing different policy options, selecting the most effective initiative, and then gradually expanding its scope. The second one is about focusing on the effectiveness of the policies irrespective of their origin and orientation. For example, China have been gradually integrated into the global economy but very cautious in capital account liberalization and retained policy space to support industrial development. Some of the critical lessons which emerge from the industrial policy experience of China are:

First, the state has a vital role in the industrialization process, which cannot be left to the market alone. The state needs to set its goals and then implement policies to enable the domestic producers to achieve those goals. For example, in the mid-1980s, the government developed and used policy guidance with specific policy measures to channel inward FDI into productive sectors, which have been proven quite successful.

Second, the state needs to constantly identify the areas that will generate the highest possible productivity and economic and social returns and keep reallocating the resources accordingly. For example, in the early 1980s, the government pushed the resources towards the light industry, particularly textiles. However, in the late-1980s, the push shifted towards energy and transportation to increase productivity across the sectors. In the early-1990s, infrastructure and high-tech industries were given support. Since 2001, resources have been reallocated towards high-tech, information, equipment manufacturing, renewable energy, and other "strategic emerging" industries essential for digital transformation.

Third, technological upgrading can play a pivotal role in the success of an industrial policy. For China, technological upgrading has always been a high priority area supported by updated laws and regulations, supportive institutions, and evolving strategies that have shifted over time from importing 'applicable technology' to developing 'national R&D capacity' to promote 'self-innovation. Along with the changing focus of the strategy, China has constantly updated its policy tools concerning imports of machinery and equipment, developing high-tech parks, revolutionizing talent strategy, and developing digital innovation hubs.

Fourth, and finally, China's successful structural transformation highlights the importance of an integrated and mutually reinforcing approach towards policy intervention. While the industrial policy has been the key to China's transformation, it would not have succeeded without a whole set of integrally coordinated development policies in trade, education, science, technology, macroeconomy, finance, digital economy, among other areas. Altogether, these policies helped to create a virtuous circle of growth and transformation.

7.4 Learning from China's Trade Policy Especially Focusing on Climbing the GVCs

China's rising share in global trade and its upgrading in global value chains from assembly lines to leading firms is inspirational for many developing countries. China not only emerged as a global manufacturing hub but became a major trading partner for many developing and developed countries. China's rising integration into the GVCs were neither automatic nor straightforward. Instead, it was a result of a well-coordinated strategic approach with the main objective of productive integration.

It is well established that linking into GVCs alone cannot guarantee the capture of significant development dividends. It requires developing productive capacities in synchronization with those needed in the GVCs. It also needs to adopt trade and industrial policies tailored to local conditions but tuned to biases and asymmetries in the external environment to avoid narrow specialization and overdependence on MNEs. In this context, China provides some handy insights for developing countries using GVCs for structural transformation, which would help further productive integration. Some of the lessons for developing countries are the following:

First, China did not simply aim at linking into GVCs but had an ambitious and strategic approach to harness increasing participation in GVCs to its developmental goals. Namely, at first, China focused on becoming a processing and assembly hub and later transforming itself into an innovation centre and a global supplier of research and development intensive parts and components. This process happened gradually and with experimentation. In the last 40 years, China has adapted its policies and moved away from preferential policies, such as taxation, conceding land and financial access to attract foreign direct investment, among other policies. After joining the WTO, China gradually reduced tariffs and facilitated investments and trade, simultaneously speeding up its reform on the public administration and delegation of power. Overall, the opening-up strategy shifted from linking into GVCs to upgrading through technological advancements and finally to setting up of China's headquartered GVCs and regional value chains.

Second, China encouraged inward and outward foreign direct investments, which helped the country upgrade its position in the GVCs. Inward FDI was encouraged to diversify from light manufacturing towards high-tech industries through the gradual use of the Catalogue of Industries to Encourage Investment. Since 2003, China has been encouraging outward FDI from China which has benefitted from its Belt and Road Initiative.

Third, China has taken full advantage of its demography and has used its abundance of labour to improve its position in the international division of labour. Besides, China has invested heavily in its transport and information infrastructures and used its industrial policy to climb the position in the international value chains.

Fourth, last but not least, China has progressively built a national innovation system by continuously increasing its science, technology, and human capital investments. These investments helped the country to narrow down its digital divide with advanced countries.

7.5 Learning from China's Digital Transformation

China's digital transformation has been exemplary for developing countries, and many lessons can be learnt from its digital policy experience. One striking feature of China's digital transformation is that, with strategic policies, this country has implemented a comprehensive national digital policy supported at sub-national and sectoral levels. Both demand and supply sides have been catered to in the digital policy along with the emphasis on developing a digital ecosystem for facilitating the operations of big and small firms.

Given China's unique political and economic realities, while it may not be possible for developing countries to replicate policies that helped in China's digital transformation, some key policy lessons can be drawn from the successful implementation of these policies.

First, China did not emulate the West when designing its policies for promoting digitalization but designed its policies to suit its ground realities. It focused on building its digital infrastructure, prioritizing ICT infrastructure and ICT skills of its population, increasing the demand and supply of ICT products and services. It then connected ICT infrastructure with manufacturing and shifted its focus on sectoral interventions.

Second, China understood the importance of data in the digital economy and therefore started designing policies to regulate its data flows. It put in place data protection laws and regulations and created data localization policies for developing its data centers to store and process its data.

Third, going beyond ICT infrastructure, China slowly but steadily built its digital infrastructure in all its provinces with support from the Centre, including broadband, cloud computing and data infrastructures. It also put in place detailed policies to encourage digital innovations and start-ups in all sectors.

Fourth, China elaborated e-commerce policies to encourage the growth of digital platforms and assisted them in becoming super platforms by providing necessary logistical support and developing an online digital payment system.

Successful implementation of digital policies in China can largely be attributed to policy coherence and policy coordination among Ministries and provinces. Strategic interventions in all sectors of the economy to progress have also played an essential role in China's digital transformation.

7.6 Learning from China's Debt Sustainability for Structural Transformation

One of the crucial learnings from China's structural transformation experience concerns its approach to internal and external debt, which is understood as a policy instrument and not as a burden to growth. China's debt sustainability policies provide useful lessons for other developing countries. Some of them are highlighted below.

First, China used debt for well-targeted investment projects, especially infrastructure projects, that expanded market boundaries and generated revenues ensuring fiscally sustainable growth. Investing in long-term, capital-intensive infrastructure projects with diverse cash flow patterns and varying social benefits allowed cash-flow smoothing.

Second, local governments, development banks, and commercial institutions worked together to finance development projects. Public and private partnerships were promoted as an alternative financing model, and accordingly, PPP industrial investment funds, special bonds for PPPs, and trading platforms of PPP assets were established, within the on-going strategic oversight of the state.

Third, public development banks like China Development Bank played an important role in providing finance and providing policy oversight on infrastructure projects to align them with the country's long-term planning. Policy banks' role mitigated the risks on development projects for commercial institutions, enabling them to provide public goods.

Fourth, China has always preferred relying on domestic rather than external debt for debt sustainability. Accordingly, the central government has always played a key role in balancing economic growth and debt management. However, the condition for a stable and sustainable debt has not been the size of debt stock to GDP, nor the scale of debt servicing to exports or reserves. Instead, the condition was the capacity to borrow in domestic credit markets and balance the annual debt servicing cost with tax revenues. Maintaining a balance between economic growth and debt accumulation ensures that the growth is robust enough to ensure sustainable debt-servicing, which is an essential learning for developing countries.

7.7. Way Forward for the Developing Countries.

After the Covid-19 pandemic is over, developing countries will have to rebuild their economies. With limited financial resources, the only option will be to provide additional policy support to their domestic producers. For this, it becomes vital for developing countries to reassess their existing macroeconomic, financial, trade, and industrial policies to recover better from the pandemic with more equitable and inclusive growth. However, for this growth to be sustainable in the digital era, appropriate digital policies need to be put in place to build their digital infrastructure. While the rising ratios of debt to GDP, provide a significant challenge to developing countries without adequate growth, ultimately it is the debt to export ratios that will constrain their capacity to service external debt. Debt should be used as a policy tool for robust growth.

Developing countries can draw many lessons from China's policies that facilitated its transformation from an agrarian economy to a global manufacturing hub and then to an emerging global digital leader. This book provides an in-depth analysis of the policies implemented by China in the areas of macroeconomic, finance, trade, industry, digital economy, and debt sustainability. Further, it provides key lessons for developing countries which can help to promote structural transformation. While China's policies cannot be replicated, they can be adjusted to address the constraints and realities of developing countries to help progress towards their sustainable development goals.

References

Andreoni, A., and Chang, H.-J. (2016), 'Industrial policy and the future of manufacturing', Journal of Industrial and Business Economics, 43(4), pp. 491-502.

Banga R and Kozul-Wright R (2018), "South-South Digital Cooperation for Industrialization; A Regional Integration Agenda", UNCTAD.

Braunstein, E., Kozul-Wright, R. and P. Fortunato (2019), "Trade and investment in the era of hyperglobalization", in: *The Palgrave Handbook of Development Economics*.

Brautigam, D (2019), A critical look at Chinese 'debt-trap diplomacy': the rise of a meme. *Area Development and Policy*. https://www.tandfonline.com/doi/full/10.1080/23792949.2019.1689828

Burlamaqui, L (2015), Finance, Development and the Entrepreneurial State: Schumpeter; Keynes; Minksy and China: *The present and Future Development of Financial institutions*; ed Burlamaqui, L, Sobreira, R and Vianna, M. MINDS: Rio de Janeiro.

Cao, Xijing and Yuan, Zhibin (2019), Overview of the Important Science and Technology Policy of New China in Past 7 Decades, *Science & Technology Review*, 37(18)Central Bank of Sri Lanka (2019), *Annual report*, vol 1.

Chang, Ha-Joon (2002), "Kicking Away the Ladder: Development Strategy in Historical Perspective," Anthem Press, London, 2002.

Cherif, Reda and Hasanov, Fuad (2019), The Return of the Policy That Shao Not Be Named: Principles of Industrial Policy, IMF Working Paper.

Ethiopian Ministry of Finance (2018), *Annual Public Sector Debt Portfolio Report* (2017/18) No.19.

Financial Times (2021). Xi Jinping's Evergrande dilemma has repercussions far beyond China, 18 October. https://www.ft.com/content/d9ce37d7-1999-4fcd-ade3-64657ea32320

Fortunato, P. and Razo, C. (2014), "Export sophistication, growth and the middle-income trap", in: Nübler, I., Salazar-Xirinachs, J.M. and R. Kozul-Wright (ed.), Transforming Economies: Making Industrial Policy Work for Growth, Jobs and Development. Geneva: International Labour Office and UNCTAD, pp. 267–287.

Gallagher KP and Zarsky (2007), The Enclave Economy: Foreign Investment and Sustainable Development in Mexico's Silicon Valley. Cambridge, MA, MIT Press.

Global capital (2019), Pakistan strives to hold on to its emerging market status. 28 March https://www.globalcapital.com/special-reports?issueid=b1dpxbhjqbxpqj&article=b1dpynz1vsr39w#:~:text=Pakistan per cent20returned per cent20to per cent20the per cent20MSCI,decade per cent20as per cent20a per cent20frontier per cent20market.&text=The per cent20country per cent20was per cent20first per cent20named,during per cent20the per cent20global per cent20financial per cent20crisis. Accessed 26 October 2020.

Gu, Mu (1978), Report on the Visit to Five Countries of Western Europe, published in the Party Literature, Vol.1, 2009.

Gul, A (2019), China: BRI Investments Boost Pakistan Economic Structure https://www.voanews.com/south-central-asia/china-bri-investments-boost-pakistan-economic-structure, accessed 2 November 2020.

Hanson, G.H (2005), Comment. in T.H. Moran, E.M. Graham and M Blomstrom (eds.) Does Foreign Direct Investment Promote Development? Washington, DC: Institute for International Economics.

Hausmann, R., Hwang, J., and D. Rodrik (2007), 'What you export matters', Journal of Economic Growth, 12(1): 1-25. Hausmann, Ricardo and Rodrik, Dani (2003), Economic Development as Self-discovery, *Journal of Development Economics*.

He, Wei & Sun, Xin (2020), China's Policy Practice for Digital Economy Development, https://unctad.org/system/files/official-document/BRI-Project_RP2_en.pdf, accessed August 4th, 2021.

Herrero, A and Xi, L (2014), China's debt problem: How worrisome and how to deal with it? *Observatoriode Divulgación Financiera Documento deTrabajo Número* 15 December www.iefweb.org/odf

Herrero, A G, (2020), China's short and long term outlook: Opportunities ahead, presentation to Forum for Macroeconomics and Macroeconomic Policies (FMM), 30 October 2020. https://www.boeckler.de/pdf/v_2020_10_30_garcia.pdf

Hsieh, Chang-Tai and Klenow, Peter (2009), Misallocation *and Manufacturing TFP in China and India*, The Quaterly Journal of Economics, Vol. CXXIV, Nov. 2009.

Hu, Jintao (2006): Speech on the National Science and Technology Conference, http://www.gov.cn/ldhd/2006-01/09/content_152487.htm accessed April 9th, 2020.

Issue 4IIF (2020), Progress Update on Private Sector Engagement in the G20 Debt Service Suspension Initiative (DSSI), 14 July. https://www.iif.com/Portals/0/Files/content/Regulatory/Progress%20Update%20to%20G20_vf.pdf, accessed 2 November 2020.

Jiang, Feitao and Li, Xiaoping (2018), Evolution and Development of China's Industrial Policy during the Four Decade of Reform and Opening-up, Management World, Vol. 10 (2018).

John Hopkins, (2020), China-Africa Research initiative. Ethiopia. http://www.sais-cari.org. Accessed 29 October 2020.

Khaliq, A. (2020), *Urgent debt relief need as Pakistan faces a perfect debt trap*. September. Eurodad. https://www.eurodad.org/urgent_debt_relief_needed_as_pakistan_faces_perfect_debt_trap.Kozul-Right, Richard and Poon, Danial (2019): *Lessons from East Asia: The Making of China's Developmental State*, 2019.

Kozul-Wright, R. and P. Fortunato (2019), Development Unchained: Trade and Industrialization in the Era of International Production. Global Policy 10 (1).

Kozul-Wright, R. and P. Fortunato (2015), Sustaining Industrial Development in the South. Development 58(4), 463–472.

Kozul-Wright, R. (ed.), Transforming Economies: Making Industrial Policy Work for Growth, Jobs and Development. Geneva: International Labour Office and UNCTAD, pp.181–211.

Lamy, P (2006) "Humanizing globalization", speech Santiago de Chile, 30 January, WTO website.Matsuyama, Kiminori (1992), *Agricultural Productivity, Comparative Advantage, and Economic Growth*, Journal of Economic Theory.

Liu, Fengchao & Sun, Yutao (2007), The Process, Trend and Suggestions of The Transformation of the Country's Scientific Policy to Innovation Policy, China Soft Science, Vol.5, pp34-42, 2007.

Matsuyama, Kiminori (1992), Agricultural Productivity, Comparative Advantage, and Economic Growth, Journal of Economic Theory, 1992.

Mazzucato, M and Wray, R. (2015), Financing the Capital Development of the Economy: A Keynes-Schumpeter-Minsky Synthesis. *LEM Working paper Series*, 14/2015. May.

Mazzucato, M. and Penna, C. (2014), "Beyond Market Failures. The Market Creating and Shaping Roles of State Investment Banks." University of Sussex Policy Research Unit Working Paper No. 2014-21.

McMillan, Margaret and Rodrik, Dani (2011), Globalization, Structural Change and Productivity Growth, NBER Working Paper 17143, 2011,

OECD (2013), Interconnected economies: Benefiting from global value chains – Synthesis Report. Paris: OECD.

Paus, E. (2014), Industrial development strategies in Costa Rica: When structural change and domestic capability accumulation diverge', in: Nübler, I., Salazar-Xirinachs, J.M. and Pavlinek, P. "Whose success? The state-foreign capital nexus and the development of the automotive industry in Slovakia". European Urban and Regional Studies.

Pavlinek, P. and J. Zenka (2016), "Value creation and value capture in the automotive industry: Empirical evidence from Czechia." Environment and Planning, 48(5): 937–959.

Plank, L. and C. Staritz (2013), "Precarious upgrading in electronics global production networks in Central and Eastern Europe: The cases of Hungary and Romania." Working Paper No. 31, Capturing the Gains, Manchester: 1–28.

Rodrik, Dani (2016), Premature Deindustrialization, Journal of Economic Growth (2016) 21: 1033.

Rodrik, Dani (2008), Second-Best institutions, American Economic Review, 2008, 98:2.

Staritz C., Plank, L., and M. Morris (2016), 'Global value chains, industrial policy and sustainable development in Ethiopia's textile and apparel export sector', Unpublished report. State bank of Pakistan. (2020), Pakistan's debt and liabilities summary. July. https://www.sbp.org.pk/ecodata/Summary.pdf. Accessed 28 October 2020.

Sun, L (2019), The structure and sustainability of China's debt. *Cambridge Journal of Economics*, 43, 695-716.

Toporowski, J. (2021 forthcoming), 'The Transfer Theory of Government Debt: What Keynes Learned from Kalecki' in P. Hawkins and I. Negru (eds.) *Monetary Economics, Banking and Policy: Expanding Economic thought to meet contemporary challenges.* Routledge.

UNCTAD (2014), Trade and Development Report, 2014: Global governance and policy space for development. New York and Geneva: United Nations Publication.

UNCTAD (2015), Global Value Chains and South-South Trade. New York and Geneva: United Nations Publication.UNCTAD (2016) Trade and Development Report, 2016: Structural Transformation for Inclusive and Sustained Growth. New York and Geneva: United Nations Publication

UNCTAD (2020a), The COVID-19 shock to developing countries: Towards a "whatever it takes" programme for the two-thirds of the world's population being left behind. United Nations. Geneva.

UNCTAD (2020b), From the Great Lockdown to the Great Meltdown: Developing Country Debt in the Time of Covid-19. United Nations. Geneva.

UNCTAD (2020c), South-south co-operation in the time of COVID-19: Building solidarity among developing countries. United Nations. Geneva.

UNCTAD (2016), Trade and development Report: Structural Transformation for Inclusive and Sustained Growth. United Nations. Geneva.

US Treasury (2020), G7 Finance Ministers' Statement on the Debt Service Suspension Initiative and Debt Relief for vulnerable countries. 25 September. https://home.treasury.gov/news/press-releases/sm1135 accessed 2 November 2020.

Wade, R. (2003), "What strategies are viable for developing countries today? The WTO and the shrinking of evelopment space", Review of International Political Economy, 10(4).

Wei, Jigang (2021), China's Industrial Policy: Evolution and Experience, https://unctad.org/system/files/official-document/BRI-Project_RP11_en.pdf, accessed December 17, 2021.

Wei, Shang-Jin; Xie, Zhuan and Zhang, Xiaobo (2016), From "Made in China" to "Innovated in China": Necessity, Prospect, and Challenges, NBER Working Paper 22854, 2016.

Wignaraja, G, Panditaratne, D, Kannangara, D and Hundlani, D. (2020), Chinese Investment and the BRI in Sri Lanka. March. Chatham House: Asia-Pacific Programme.

WTO, Fung Global Institute and Nanyang Technological University (2013), Global Value Chains in a Changing World. Geneva: World Trade Organization.

ZHANG, B and Lu, T. (2019), *Debt sustainability and Debt Management: Lessons from China*. Background paper prepared for UNCTAD's project "South-South Integration and the SDGs: Enhancing Structural Transformation in Key Partner Countries of the Belt and Road Initiative". October.

Zhao, Ying (2012), Empirical Study of the Changing Trend of China's Industrial Policy:2000-2010, Economic Management Publisher, 2012.